THE NORTH KOREAN THREAT AND CHINESE FOREIGN POLITICS WITH NORTH KOREA

PEKING KING

THE NORTH KOREAN THREAT AND CHINESE FOREIGN POLITICS WITH NORTH KOREA

iUniverse books may be ordered through booksellers or by contacting:

iUniverse
1663 Liberty Drive
Bloomington, IN 47403
www.iuniverse.com
1-800-Authors (1-800-288-4677)

Because of the dynamic nature of the Internet, any web addresses or links contained in this book may have changed since publication and may no longer be valid. The views expressed in this work are solely those of the author and do not necessarily reflect the views of the publisher, and the publisher hereby disclaims any responsibility for them.

Any people depicted in stock imagery provided by Getty Images are models, and such images are being used for illustrative purposes only. Certain stock imagery © Getty Images.

ISBN: 978-1-5320-6299-5 (sc)
ISBN: 978-1-5320-6300-8 (hc)
ISBN: 978-1-5320-6301-5 (e)

Library of Congress Control Number: 2018914352

Print information available on the last page.

iUniverse rev. date: 12/04/2018

A Stunning Rumor of the Invasion

One day, I was in the conference room of an airport and there was a group of government officials starting the discussion. The discussion was not official. Just like people discussing football or baseball games on break time. This has nothing to do with the government's decision, but the private opinion for some influential individual.

Scott, a senior official who used to serve in the Vietnam War, the First Gulf War in 1991, and the Second Gulf War in 2003, just came home from the Middle East war zone and said:

"The North Korean military, backed by the Chinese military, with millions of troops, thousands of aircrafts, and hundreds of warships, will start the war against South Korea and our troops in South Korea and the entire Far East within weeks.

In the recent days, there has been an unusual movement across the border from North Korea. Several armies of the Chinese military moved closer to the border with North Korea. There has been an increased number of warships and aircrafts activity near the Korean peninsula.

We must prepare for the war against the Chinese and the North Koreans invasion. The second Korean War will start very soon, possibly within the next few weeks."

In the conference room, all the people agreed with his opinion and joined the discussion. The only one having the opposite opinion is me. I'm a Chinese descendant who has stayed in America for 35 years. I said:

Pardon me, ladies and gentlemen, I don't believe there will be a war starting in Korea at any time in the near future. The Korean War has been over for over 60 years. Xi Jinping is not Mao Zedong. Kim Jung-Un is not Kim Il Sung. And Putin is not Stalin. The Cold War has been over for two generations. We should forget the past, since those Cold War-era communist politicians are all dead and buried. Please update our political knowledge. There is no way Kim Jung-Un will start a war soon.

Of course, we will see a lot of media outlets exaggerate the threats. Those are fake news and they do not exist. Remember during the Cold War era when there were a lot of rumors that the Soviet Union would take over Western Europe? It never happened.

To no surprise, everybody in the room disagreed with me. The discussion continued and I said:

"The real reason the Chinese military moved closer to the North Korean border is not they want to support North Korea for the invasion, but to give Kim Jung-Un a warning. The warning was not sent either to South Korea or the American troops, but as a warning to the North Korean regime.

If Kim Jong-Un dares to start a war, millions of North Korean refugees will flee the country and try to cross the border into China. But the Chinese government does not allow it or welcome them. If they cross the border, the Chinese military will not allow them to enter. It is the real reason."

As per my prediction, I was right about that. The war never started. My only regret is I was pretty sure I was right. I should have placed a bet on it. Surprisingly, not only does the general public in America not understand the Chinese and North Korean regimes, likewise the government officials. There are secrets about both governments outside the world who never know about it.

Let me tell you a trick to getting information from an enemy country that doesn't welcome the American media. If they don't allow the American journalists to visit their country and you want to get any information from this hostile country, the easiest way is to get the secondhand information from their allies.

North Korea is the world's most hated American enemy excluding Iran. They don't like Americans as well as anyone from Canada and Western Europe. Just like Iran, they are not just anti-American, but anti-west. The Chinese are the closest ally for North Korea. Why can't we just get second-hand information from the Chinese media?

I am fully bilingual and able to read both the Chinese and English internet. There have been discussions about if Kim Jong-Un will dare to start the Korean War, how will the Chinese government respond? If they act low-key, they will just close the border, and stop the refugees as well as the North Korean officials from getting into China.

If they act obtrusive, the Chinese troops will cross the border to take over the major key facilities such as the nuclear weapons storage and missile launch sites. They don't want the North Koreans to use their weapons of mass destruction against their ally, which is South Korea.

For China, South Korea is a more important ally than North Korea. There are many different kinds of allies. North Korea is a political ally for Russia and China but not a military ally anymore. South Korea, despite not being either a political or military ally for China, is one of the most important economic, science, and technological allies. There are major investments and trade between China and South Korea.

China is one of the world's biggest economy (depending on what is the standard. Some source say that America is the world's biggest economy and China is the second). South Korea is the world's 11th biggest economy, and have a higher GDP than Russia (According to the International Monetary Fund, 2017 GDP). Both of them have a fast growing GDP.

There are hundreds of billions of dollars the trade between each country annually. North Korea is one of the world's poorest countries. After the Cold War ended, the economic alliance between China and North Korea also ended. If the second Korean War begins, the North Korean regime will have to fight alone without the help from either China or Russia. A lot of the money the Chinese invested in South Korea will vanish. The Chinese government certainly does not want to see a second Korean War.

The Chinese government has a totally different idea regarding foreign policy. The rest of the world hardly understands what they are trying to do. They have no interest in protecting, or fight for North Korea because North Korea is not their economic ally. What they like to do is protect their trade and money in South Korea. They would lose too much economically if war were to break out.

Imagine having two neighbors who live by your house. One is a poor beggar who has major financial problems and frequently begs you for money. His grandfather was a very good friend of your grandfather.

Your other neighbor had a grandfather who was enemies with your grandfather. Now, he is a wealthy businessman and the two of you are getting along and have become business partners. Besides that, your rich neighbor has a friend whose name is USA. He is a very wealthy man and he is another one of your business partners.

Your poor neighbor takes a gun and threatens to shoot both your rich neighbor and his friend. Who would you hope wins? If you don't want to get involved, you could close the door and pretend you're not in the middle of the conflict or simply sneak up from behind him and snatch his gun.

In the recent years the Chinese military budget has increased rapidly, especially the navy. They are building more and "major surface ships" and submarines than any countries including America. The Chinese manufacturing J-20 stealth fighters, which is the worlds most advanced fighter except for the American F-22. The amphibian landing capability also increased rapidly. A lot of people have the belief that to conquer a large island you must have a powerful navy, air force and amphibian landing capabilities. People may think if it is possible it is prepared to invade Taiwan.

Here is the rumor, popular but false. There is an agreement between China and North Korea. When North Korea invaded the South, China will launch amphibian attacks against Taiwan at the same time. It makes America and his allies unable to juggle two wars.

Unlike decades ago, since the economic reform began in the late 1970's, China and South Korea started a powerful trade and business alliance. In the opposite side, China approved and joined the sanctions against North Korea. The Chinese government is not going to destroy powerful trade and business alliance to help its poor neighbor.

The later part of the book there is an exclusive article to talk about trade and political policy about which the Chinese government and both Koreas and Taiwan.

I have a habit to review military and political articles and stories every day in articles and internet. At least once a week I visit bookstores. Unbelievable, very big majority of American people have little or no knowledge about either political issues or military activity that happens in Eastern Asia. You could go to bookstore and internet to review books and magazines and internet articles published by famous publishers. Those authors could be politicians, professors or military officials. Their minds are stuck in the Cold War era, and calling themselves Eastern Asia experts. Their opinions are outdated nonsense.

Unlike science and technologies people like new equipment upgraded, such as an IPhone. When you have an IPhone 6, you would like to upgrade to an IPhone 7. When you have an IPhone 7 you want to upgrade it to an IPhone 8, or IPhone X. Peoples foreign political knowledge should be just be upgraded just like a cell phone.

Why China was Involved
in the Wars in Asia

Westerners do not understand the history of Eastern Asia. Through the history, **Korea and Vietnam were Chinese protected states.** In the recent history, not exactly the same but similar to satellite states between the Eastern European nations and the Soviet Union. If somebody dared to invade countries such as Poland or East Germany, Russia would join the war.

One of the major differences is although everybody knows the Eastern European countries have Russia as their overlord, on paper they are independent nations. They are equals. The relationship between China and Korea and Vietnam were officially that of a superior and subordinate. As an example, the ruler of China was called the emperor. The ruler of Korea and Vietnam were not allowed to be called emperors, but kings. When the ambassadors from Korea and Vietnam went to see the emperor of China, the Chinese government would treat them like subordinates who send envoys to see their superiors. Japan was never a Chinese protected nation. As a result, the ruler of Japan can still be called the emperor. When the ambassador representing the Japanese emperor went to see the Chinese emperor, it would be seen as an equal nation-to-nation meeting.

Throughout history, China was the oldest, biggest, and most influential nation is East Asia. Korea and Vietnam had populations and sizes similar to a large province in China. There were many immigrants from China to both countries. Even today, if you went to an Asian supermarket, you may find something interesting. The store owner could be Korean or Vietnamese, yet they may learn how to speak Chinese. You will never see a Chinese store owner learn to speak Korean or Vietnamese. The Chinese are traditionally their superiors and bosses.

In 1046 BC, the last ruler of the Chinese Shang Dynasty was overthrown by the Zhou Dynasty. One of the noblemen in Shang Dynasty, Gija, together with 3000 Chinese people, left China and immigrated to Korea to form their own nation. In 194 BC, another nobleman named Wiman left China with his army to conquer Korea. During the Han Dynasty, Korea was conquered by the Chinese. After Han Dynasty collapsed, Korea became an independent nation. A few hundred years later, Korea was conquered again by the Chinese Tang Dynasty. After Tang Dynasty collapsed, Korea became an independent nation again.

Joseon Dynasty (1392 to 1897) was one of the longest lasting dynasties in Korea and the last dynasty before they were conquered by the Japanese. The Ming and Qing emperors were officially the superiors to the Joseon Dynasty's kings.

In 1592, the Japanese samurai invaded Korea. Korea is a smaller and less populated nation, incapable of defending themselves. The Korean ambassador went to Beijing asking for help. The Korean ambassador laid down on the front steps of the Forbidden City wailing, begging the emperor of China to send armies to save Korea. Wanli Emperor was sympathetic enough to save Korea. He deployed the Ming army and navy to Korea to fight the Japanese.

I used to watch television shows which exaggerate, stating that the Japanese samurai were good fighters. The program producers must be incapable of reading Asian history books. During the war, the Japanese had a slight advantage in terms of manpower. 300,000 Japanese against the Korean and Chinese, who had the combined forces of 250,000. The Ming military defeated the Japanese samurai.

A few years later, the Japanese invaded Korea again and the Ming army and navy were able to defeat them again. After the war ended, the Korean king promised loyalty to the Ming Dynasty forever, even after the Ming Dynasty collapsed.

Despite this, in 1644, the Ming Dynasty was overthrown by the Qing Dynasty. Officially, the king of Korea was still loyal to the Ming government. If you see a picture of a Korean king, he dresses exactly like the Ming emperor. The Korean government officials had an identical dress code to the Ming Dynasty officials.

In 1894, the Japanese invaded Korea. The Korean government immediately asked the Qing government to help fight the Japanese. Unfortunately, during the late Qing Dynasty, the Chinese government, including the military, were corrupt. Both the Chinese and Korean military were defeated. As a result, the Japanese occupied Korea until 1945.

The situation in Vietnam was quite similar to Korea. Vietnam was conquered by the Chinese multiple times. During the Ming Dynasty, Vietnam was also a country protected by China.

In 1400, The Vietnamese King Tran Thieu De was overthrown. He went to Beijing and cried to the Ming Emperor Wing Lok(Yongle). The Chinese emperor ordered to invade Vietnam. After the Chinese won the war, they conquered Vietnam. In 1427, the Chinese Government set a deal with Vietnam. The Chinese approved to have one of the princes of Vietnam become the King of Vietnam. The Chinese troops retreated. The Chinese emperor is recognized as the superior to the King of Vietnam.

Just like Korea, Vietnam was loyal to the Ming Dynasty. The imperial Vietnamese king dressed exactly like the Chinese emperor. The Vietnamese government officials dressed exactly like the Ming Dynasty government officials.

One interesting fact about Vietnam. The Vietnamese Government officials call their ruler as "emperor", if there are no foreigners around. If foreign diplomate around they downgrade the title to "king".

After the Ming Dynasty was overthrown and the Qing Dynasty formed, they inherited Korea and Vietnam as their protected country. In 1884, the French military invaded Vietnam. The Chinese Government declared war on France. The Qing army and navy were defeated. As a result, Vietnam became a French colony until after WWII, the Vietnamese people pushed back the French.

Communist China believed that they inherited Korea and Vietnam as their protected countries, as well other lands such as Spratly Islands, Xinjiang and Tibet and Taiwan. Throughout history, China governed those regions for hundreds of years. When other nations interfere in their conflicts, they are considered to be "imperial invaders" trying to stop them from being united.

The Chinese family caste system is very powerful and still influences the entire Eastern Asia. The Chinese Government is treating Korea and Vietnam and other smaller neighbor nations as their nephews, not younger brothers.

The rank of a Chinese family has the older siblings as a higher rank than younger siblings. Uncles and aunts are higher ranking than their nephews and nieces. When their little nephews and nieces are attacked by other families (such as America), their uncle has to stand up to back their little relatives.

When I tell my friends the above stories, they ask if Ming Dynasty was such a powerful country, why not the Ming Emperors don't just take over and conquer Korea and Vietnam? Of course I wish I could turn back time and make Korea and Vietnam annexed by China. If there is a case, it will eliminate some international bloody conflict. It would be no Korean War and Vietnam War. Why the Chinese didn't annex them?

The Han ethnic is the majority ethnic group and mainstream of the Chinese culture. It is also the most civilized and oldest ethnic group. The Han ethnic group are peaceful and against Imperialism. Genghis Khan was of Mongolian ethnic descent and he had a different culture than the Han.

When Ming Dynasty was in its strongest period, they had the military power to conquer the entire East Asia. It did not happen because the Ming Emperor was of Han ethnicity, the same as Xi Jinping and most Chinese officials today. If you do not interfere with their national businesses and political issues, they could be your good friend. If they feel threatened by you, they could retaliate harshly.

How the Chinese View
Themselves and Others

China has a very splendid history. Unlike the Roman Empire, after the Western Roman Empire collapsed, you will not see a very great empire in the western world until now. The Chinese has the world's highest GDP and the most advanced technology between Han Dynasty (206 BC-220 AD) until the early 19th century, when the Americans and Europeans began the industrial revolution. Although somebody will dispute me about such claim, all the Chinese people believe it. Their downfall was not their own fault, but the fault of their imperialist enemies distributing them opium and poisoning them and invading them with military power. Today, the Chinese attempt to reclaim their title again.

The name '中國' means 'Middle Kingdom' in Chinese. The reason is because they believed they were in the center of the world. The other name of the Chinese ruler is called 'The Son of Heaven'. Let me explain what that really means. God lives in the heavens. Jesus Christ is the son of God. The true meaning of Son of Heaven is the ruler of China is called 'Jesus Christ'. It is the most beautiful and powerful title on Earth.

Because of her size, population, wealth, and technology, in tradition, China was the big boss in Asia. In 1840, the British imperials invaded China and started the First Opium War. After China's defeat in the war, the imperial invaders took advantage of the weakness of the Qing Government, such as the soldiers taking drugs, the government officials taking bribes, all their little nephews were conquered by invaders. The British took Burma, the French took Vietnam, Laos, and Cambodia, Japan took Korea, and the Russians took Outer Mongolia. According to most Chinese people, the Japanese and the Europeans are foreign invaders.

After the Japanese took over Korea in 1894, the imperial Korean Government became their puppet state. In 1910, when the Japanese Government believed they no longer had problems to fight the resistance, they annexed Korea and made her Japanese territory.

Across the border from Korea is Manchuria, which is Chinese territory. In 1931, the Japanese invaded Manchuria. After they conquered Manchuria, the last emperor of China, Pu Yi (who was actually overthrown in 1912) travelled to Manchuria and declared himself as the emperor of Manchuria, which was a puppet government under Japanese control. The 1987 movie "The Last Emperor" is based on this story.

Once the Japanese controlled Manchuria, the Japanese attempted to conquer the entire China. In 1937, the Japanese started a full scale war against China. The bloodiest fight caused the deaths of tens of millions of Chinese people, continuing until the Japanese surrendered in 1945.

In 1950, the United Nations joint forces, led by America, was winning the war. The North Korean military was facing defeat. When the war was moved closer and closer to the Chinese border, the Chinese Communist government decided to rescue North Korea and join the war.

General MacArthur was a good general, but had no political insight or knowledge. He believed the America has to win the Korean War and defeat the communists. So the war was expanded to Manchuria. Thanks to President Truman firing of General MacArthur immediately, and sent him back to America. The Korean War was limited in the Korean Peninsula. President Truman's successor President Eisenhower followed the idea of a limited war. The war was over in 1953.

I reviewed a lot of articles posted on the Chinese internet. Back to the 1950's, after the North Korean military was defeated by America and her allies, and the war was getting closer to the Chinese border, there was a common belief for most Chinese people that the Americans, after defeating the North Korean communists, would conquer Korea just like the Japanese did. They would than follow the same steps and invade Manchuria. After the Americans conquered Manchuria, they would start a full scale war in an attempt to conquer China, very similar to what the Japanese used to do. If we have to defend China, we must defend our protected country, Korea, first.

While this idea was not true, it was a common belief amongst the Chinese people. As a result, the Communist Chinese took military action and deployed troops to fight in the Korean War, just like the Ming Dynasty and Qing Dynasty deployed troops into Korea to fight the Japanese invaders.

In reality, the U.S. Government never had a plan to spread the war to China. The only purpose is the American Government wants to stop the communists expand their territories. When the Korean War began in 1950, it was just five years after the end of WWII. The people in Asia when they think about a western country would believe there are the imperialist invaders. There were very few Asians living in America at that time. When American troops were deployed to Asia they may treat every Asians as enemies. Just like the Japanese they fought in the Pacific War. Although it was a mistake in communication, since the mistake had been made, the hostilities continued for a several decades.

In Eastern Asia, treating the Americans and their European allies as foreign invaders is a common belief set in stone. There was Japanese propaganda during WWII when the Japanese started the Pacific War stating they would conquer every country in Eastern Asia. The reason is the Japanese Government wanted to free all of the countries in Eastern Asia from the American and European imperial invaders. After each country was conquered, they created a puppet government under Japanese control. As an example, the Empire of Vietnam. If America did not win the fight against Japan, I believe a few years later, the emperor of Vietnam would be forced to abdicate and the Japanese would annex Vietnam just like they did for Korea.

During the Vietnam War, the Chinese supported North Vietnam with weapons food and equipment, based on the same reasoning. Thanks to President Truman and his successor Eisenhower, has the same fore site. To limit the Korean War so it would not spread to China. If the war expanded to China, not just increase the hostilities between China and America, the Chinese people would treat Americans as national enemies, just like some European nation felt toward Nazi Germany. As a result, the Chinese would deploy the real army, navy and air force to join active combat in Vietnam. The Vietnam War would become even more deadly and high cost.

Even today, the Chinese Government and most of the Chinese people do not understand or trust Westerners, especially Americans. Here is a list of ongoing conflicts:

After WWII, the Chinese Nationalist government was seriously weakened. They lost the war against the Communists. As a result, the Nationalist Government officials left the mainland and moved to Taiwan. The new nation created by the Chinese communist called "The People's Republic of China". The Taiwanese Government called "The Republic of China". They sound almost the same, and sometimes confuses people.

When the People's Republic of China just formed, communist China did not have a large navy and an amphibious invasion force powerful enough to take military Taiwan. And the US Navy was protecting Taiwan, the communists did not take over Taiwan. The Nationalists formed their own government in Taiwan. Officially, Taiwan is not a nation, but a province. There is an ongoing political argument between America and China about Taiwan. For instance if a diplomate referred to Taiwan as "The Republic of China", it is unacceptable.

Today, mainland China and Taiwan are relatives and business partners. Because of the business benefits, China and Taiwan invest money into each other, just like China does with South Korea. There is no way China will invade Taiwan with military force, despite their powerful military force capable for a successful invasion. Because the westerners (including America) does not understand Asia, just like how Asians do not understand the west, there is fake news repeatedly published through the internet, books, and magazines.

One of the famous rumors I used to hear is absolutely fake news. The rumor is the Chinese will start an amphibious invasion against Taiwan. Simultaneously, the American military would become involved in the war against the Chinese military. Shortly after, North Korea would take advantage of the American military putting their focus in the Battle of Taiwan and start an invasion against South Korea. This fairytale was repeatedly published by the American people with no knowledge about the current situation in Asia.

The Spratly Islands were a Chinese territory since Song Dynasty (960 AD to 1279 AD). Ming Dynasty (1368 to 1644) was a golden era in Chinese history. During the Ming Dynasty, China was the lone superpower on earth. They had the world's biggest navy during the Emperor Wing Lok (Yongle) era (1402 – 1424). Nobody in Asia would dare mess with the Ming navy.

Emperor Wing Lok ordered Admiral Zheng to deploy ships into the Indian Ocean. He commanded expeditionary voyages to Southeast Asia, South Asia, Western Asia, and East Africa from 1405 to 1433. The largest ships in Zheng He's fleet named "Treasure ships" which has nine masts, about 127 meters (417 feet) long and 52 meters (171 feet) wide. During that period of time, the ship building technology all over the world was very primitive, even in Europe. I would not be surprised to hear the Chinese navy has full control of the South China Sea during the Ming Dynasty. They claim they owned the Spratly Islands for several hundred years.

When the Dutch invaded Eastern Asia and built colonies, they had several battles engaging the Ming navy. Most of the time, the Chinese won the battles. There is no doubt the history books published in China will say the Spratly Islands belong to China.

Here is the facts: Who has the biggest military power. Who would win control of the disputed territory? Of course, China has the biggest military power in the South China Sea. The Spratly Islands are claimed by five governments: China, Taiwan, Vietnam, Philippians, and Malesia. The Chinese navy is bigger than the other four added together. Not just in quantity, but quality. As an example, the newly launched Type 055 Destroyers, is the largest and most powerful combat vessel in Asia since WWII. They are the World's largest and most modern destroyers but the USN Zumwalt-class destroyers. Due to the high manufacturing cost the Americans can only afford to make three Zumwalt-class destroyers. The Chinese is able to mass produce Type 055 Destroyers.

We all know America has the world's biggest and most powerful navy. The second most powerful navy on earth belongs to China, not Russia.

Russian warships are mostly very old, built during the Cold War era, and are incapable in real combat. Most of the Chinese warships were built after the Cold War had ended. The quality of the major service ship combat vessels are superior to that of Russian warships. There is no way to stop the Chinese from building more artificial islands in the South China Sea.

In recent years, America is often sailing warships into Chinese claimed waters nearby the Chinese built artificial islands. As soon as the Chinese warships arrive, the American warships flee. Such practice does not provide gain for either side. Contrary, it creates more difficulty for the diplomates to negotiate solutions to resolve other international issues. There is no benefit to sending warships into Chinese-claimed waters. This only causes an escalation of hostilities and mistrust.

Somebody says if you "won't dare open fire-don't show me your gun." For American navy was "playing tag", in the South China seas, seemed like the American warship wanted to test their engines and mobility. However they refrained from firing power.

Tibet was never an independent nation since Yuan Dynasty (1206 to 1368). Yuan Dynasty was originally called 'Mongolian Dynasty'. Because they worship Confucius, they changed their name to Yuan Dynasty. 'Yuan' means 'beginning' in Confucius's books. The Mongolian emperor picked up such great words and made it to be the name of the dynasty.

It is a strange fact about Yuan Dynasty that the people could worship multiple religions at the same time. The national religion considered Confucius as holy, but at the same time, worshipped Buddhism or some other religion.

Before the communists took over Tibet, it was a very strange political system. Tibet had no king and no governor. The supreme ruler in Tibet was a Buddhist monk. The title of the monk is called the Dalai Lama. Today's Dalai Lama is the fourteenth Dalai Lama.

Tibet was officially a special district which belonged to China since Yuan Dynasty. Ming Dynasty inherited from Yuan Dynasty and Qing Dynasty inherited from Ming Dynasty. After Qing Dynasty was overthrown in 1912, the Republic of China inherited Tibet as well as Communist China, which today is called the People's Republic of China.

When a Dalai Lama dies, after a period of time, the Tibetan Buddhist temple would elect a new Dalai Lama. The Tibetan government would have to send an envoy to go to Beijing and ask the Emperor of China to sign an order to approve the new Dalai Lama as ruler of Tibet. Here is the trick: the official paper does not say the Emperor of China approves somebody become the Dalai Lama to rule Tibet. The paper says the Emperor of China orders somebody to become Dalai Lama and rule Tibet.

After the Communists inherited Tibet, Mao Zedong thought "What would happen if I refused to accept the Dalai Lama as the ruler of Tibet and instead I simply fire him?" The Chinese government told the Dalai Lama **"You are fired."** The 14th Dalai Lama was exiled since then. There is an iron fist to rule Tibet since then.

If you understand the interior politics of China, there is no way to make the Chinese government give up Tibet. Even the Dalai Lama understand himself. He used to say, "I am the last Dalai Lama, after I pass it will be no more Dalai Lama".

The Chinese Government does not like any foreign country to be involved with their domestic conflicts and issues. It may look like international conflicts from a western perspective, but in their minds eye, they are domestic conflicts.

Taiwan is province of China, not a nation. Republic of China should be only seen in a history book, has been replaced by The People's Republic of China since 1949. The entire South China Sea including all the islands there belong to China. Building artificial islands are not the business of foreign governments. Tibet never achieved independence since 800 years ago. The Dalai Lama was displaced by the central government. There is no foreign country has the right to lift him back into power.

Nobody have a way to make China mend their human rights violation. China non-stop to expand their artificial islands. Since they have money, manpower and technology to create or expand the artificial islands in South China Seas, and they have the air and naval powers to defend them. The operation is unstoppable. Any disagreement and complaint by the western societies would not be appreciated, but fuel hostilities.

Western societies including most high ranking politicians don't read the history or current policies but North Korea does, they have common beliefs. They appreciate each other and become political allies, (they are no longer military allies nor economical allies). The Chinese Government was deeply concerned about American military activity in the West Pacific this includes military surveillance, the naval vessels sailing nearby Chinese claimed waters, and the American missile defense system such as THAAD system deployed nearby China.

There is enormous disagreements about all the above issues circulating currently between America and China. Recently the American Government imposed tariffs on imported Chinese products, the Chinese Government immediately tariffs on the imported American products. The trade war between the world's two biggest economies has begun.

Somebody might think that North Korean issues is a separate topic which has nothing to do with the trade war. In reality the Chinese politicians want to use North Korea to be one of the cards used in gaining negotiation power. In the international disputes each of those issues seem unrelated but the politicians are using each of these disputes and they add up it is put on the negotiating table. There are secrets about negotiation that the journalists may never be able to broadcast.

As an example, in the United Nations China approved sanctions against North Korea joined by all the members of the U.N. Security Council. Since the sanctions began the trade between China and North Korea dropped dramatically. The trade between the two nations almost completely cut off. There still is limited trade between these two nations despite they violate the sanctions. As an example, after the oil embargo began, some Chinese tankers transfer fuel into the North Korean tankers in the international waters illegally. Why the Chinese are providing such little fuel to them. China wants the North Korean regime to survive but not to expand or use its military against South Korea.

Since the U.N. Security Council approved sanctions against North Korea, China and Russia never fully implemented complete sanctions. Shortly after the trade war began, the Chinese scaled down the sanctions against North Korea. I don't believe these are unrelated issues.

China may be the only country on Earth that can understand the situations of North Korea including its internal and domestic issues. They don't want to help North Korea to take over South Korea. They don't want to see communism collapse in North Korea either. They are giving North Korea a little help and never enforce a strict sanctions against North Korea, despite in the U.N. they vote for the sanction bill. They are afraid if the sanctions are too harsh on North Korea the Communist Government will collapse.

Westerner Phobia

I worked for the American Federal Government since 1991. A lot of my co-workers are veterans. Some of them are still serving in the reserves. When I just started, there were Pacific War veterans. All of them either retired or died. There were Korean War veterans. They are also gone. There is Vietnam War veterans. Most of them have retired, but some of them are still active. Gulf War veterans and some military veterans who never served a war are the majority of veterans in my agencies.

Just look at the list of wars America used to fight. There have been warrant officers and high ranking officers who became my co-workers. We often discuss war. There is one thing they will never understand, why when they were deployed overseas, the native people look at them with hate and suspicion. When I tell them my opinion, they will not believe me.

There are some major mistakes American people including even high-ranking politicians and military officials do not understand. A lot of people overseas hate Americans just as much as Europeans hate the Nazis, and the American people, including military personnel, believe everyone should love them, but deadly incidents prove them wrong.

In the eyes of Americans, the American people are liberators. We overthrew Saddam Hussein, and freed Iraq. We fought the communists, stopped their invasions, but why do the people not appreciate us helping them and saving them? Why do they treat us with such hostility?

I tell my coworkers "I believe your ideas are absolutely right. We are the liberators, but our idea will only be accepted in America and in our allies' countries, such as Canada and Western Europe. How could we convince other people who live on the other side of the world who do not speak our language and do not communicate with you? In those hostile nations, there is no freedom of press. The citizens will only listen to the propaganda published by their government."

In recent history, imperialism made the Europeans and their descendants conquer most of the world, excluding a handful of nations such as Japan, China, Thailand, Turkey, and Saudi Arabia.

When an Asian or Arab saw somebody who look like a westerner, they will immediately identify them as imperialist invaders. We do not speak their language and we do not understand them, just like how they do not speak our language or understand us.

Unfortunately, this kind of hostility continued after WWII ended. Most of the Europeans who conquered colonies became independent. After they became independent, there was civil war fighting over who got to rule these ex-colonies' nations. You don't have to be a colonial invader, but just look like one. The first response is "This is a bad guy trying to enslave us. Let's kill him."

In the past, Hong Kong was a British colony, and it is where I was born. When I was little, I eye-witnessed unfair promotions, such as a British man who worked for the Hong Kong British government could get a higher paying, higher ranking job, but his colleague who is more qualified than him would not get the promotion.

The education system in Hong Kong was a terrible nightmare. Most of the people were not able to graduate high school. The free education is only up to elementary school. When I was in high school, I often talked about wanting to go to college, and everyone thought that it was only a daydream because there are only three universities available. When the Hong Kong government had an enormous surplus, they would just send the money to England and not give to the Hong Kong people or spend it on badly needed programs, such as education. When I talked about it with other people in Hong Kong, a lot of people were angry. The "colonial government" has been helping their own people (British people) to make money and not helping the native people (Chinese people living in Hong Kong) to progress.

A lot of people told me it is very unlikely I could go to college in Hong Kong. If I want to go college, I would have to go to America. As a result, I immigrated to America after I graduated high school in Hong Kong. I was never in Vietnam before, but some of my classmates are from Vietnam.

I attended college in New York City. At that time, most of the students were either white, African American, or Hispanic. Only a few students were from Asia. We felt more comfortable socializing with our own groups. We formed a little group and talked about politics after class.

In 1884, France invaded Vietnam, a Qing protectorate. The French imperialists defeated the Vietnamese and Qing armies. In 1885, they conquered Vietnam and made it their colony. During WWII, Vietnam was occupied by Japan. Both of the invaders who occupied Vietnam did so to steal from the native people. The Vietnamese people were rebellious against the French colonists. The French often jailed or killed revolutionaries. Although the French had retreated, shortly after, the Americans joined the war. They looked just like the French and they all believed the Americans are other imperialist colonists.

There are things in western society nobody will hear or understand. **Westerner Phobia** was very common in Asia during the Cold War era. Today, due to globalization, not including North Korea, it is almost extinct in Asia. Before Japan was occupied in 1945, the Japanese also had Westerner Phobia. It may be too difficult to explain what this word means. Just to change the topic, in America, some people have Islamophobia. As I'm writing this, the president is Donald Trump. He signed a law banning immigration from some predominately Muslim countries. Surprisingly, the American Supreme Court backed his decision. That means the majority of Supreme Court justices also have Islamophobia.

Not everyone from these predominately Muslim countries have to be terrorists. If just a small number of them commit terrorist acts, they will make people uncomfortable with them. Westerner Phobia is based on a similar idea. The difference is that, if a Muslim does not dress like a traditional religious Muslim and wears modern clothing like a westerner, people won't pay attention nor label him as a terrorist. A Caucasian person has no way to pretend to not be Caucasian. When Caucasian people travel to an anti-western country, such as some Muslim majority countries in Africa, they may be met with hostility.

Another mistake the Americans made was helping the bad guys. All of my Vietnamese classmates told me the exact same story. The South Vietnamese Government was a terribly corrupt government. Everybody hated this government. They are the true enemies of the Vietnamese people. When the Americans helped such a corrupt government, the Americans became the Vietnamese' public enemies.

One of my co-workers served active duty in the Vietnam War. He told me stories. When they deployed toward a South Vietnam village, the communist rebels, including women, children, and senior citizens, picked up and fired all kinds of weapons to attack them from every direction. They found that there were guerillas as young as seven years old. They fired back, killing a lot of Vietnamese people and burned the village to the ground.

I asked my co-worker who told me the above story, "When you served combat duty in Vietnam, were you involved in the My Lai massacre?" He said he wasn't involved in the My Lai massacre but one of his buddies was. I asked, "When you served combat duty, did you ever kill anyone?" He said "I did." Then he told me the reason. "When we walked past a village, somebody kept shooting us from behind. We had no clue where the gunmen were. The only thing we knew was that there was a village nearby. We surrounded the village and ordered all of the villagers to put their hands on top of their heads and prove they did not have any weapons. The villagers were not allowed to carry anything nor walk out of the village within 15 minutes. After 15 minutes, we got into the village and killed everybody, including babies, women, and children and burned the village down." He explained to me, when you are in warzone, the most important thing is saving your own life. Of course, what the American soldiers did was not popular.

After this battle, when they deployed to other villages, again, old men, women, and children picked up any kind of weapons they had and tried to kill them. He served in battles just like this countless times. How could you believe everybody should love the Americans because Americans are their liberators and are going to free them from the communists? They called the Americans and another westerner, devils.

Somebody from Vietnam told me a story: An American soldier in Saigon walked into a day care center for young children, he was followed by an insurgent shortly afterwards a grenade was thrown through the window and landed near him. To protect the children he covered the grenade with his own body. The grenade exploded and killed him. I don't believe the person who threw the grenade wanted to kill the children. The only target was this individual solider.

All of the Korean people I know, including my classmates and coworkers, were born after the Korean War. I was told, during the Korean War, the Americans committed a similar massacre for a similar reason. Today, after several decades and three generations, the North Korean regime is still using the massacres the Americans committed during the Korean War as propaganda. Don't you think this is outdated? But the Chinese have forgotten about it. After the Cold War ended, China has become a major American trading partner and Westerner Phobia no longer exists in China.

The American people may think the communist propaganda turned the Vietnamese people against them but there was a lot more to it than that. Your enemy's friend is your enemy. The South Vietnam government was so terribly corrupt and nobody in Vietnam liked them. My Vietnamese classmates in college told me stories. During the Vietnam War, America sent countless supplies to Vietnam. When the supplies arrived in Vietnam, the South Vietnamese Government officials would steal the materials and sell them on the black market. These supplies included guns, grenades, and ammo.

Criminals purchased the weapons and committed extortion and other criminal activities. For example, one day, a handicapped man in a wheelchair said he was a veteran and went to a theatre. When he tried to get in the door, the ticket attendant stopped him and asked him for a ticket. The veteran took out a grenade from his pocket and showed it to the ticket attendant. The ticket attendant let him in without a ticket. The ticket attendant remembered other theatres were blown up by grenades not too long ago. He should understand what the grenade meant and what would happen if he didn't let him in.

My classmates were about the same age as me. I was 12 years old when the Vietnam War ended. I am lucky to not one of them. Here is another story. One of my classmates was in a South Vietnamese barrack to shine a soldier's boots. After the job was done, the soldier found that he was short on money. He gave him a couple of bullets instead. He asked the soldier "What should I do with this ammo?" He said "Do you like to play fireworks? You take out the bullet and inside the cartridge is gunpowder." My classmate was an innocent child at the time. He didn't know the danger. He took the ammo home, removed the bullet, and tried to light it up like a firework. As soon as he lit it up, he was burned, and it left a scar on his skin.

Shortly after the American military retreated, the communists took over South Vietnam and ended the war. Before the war was over, some South Vietnamese corrupt politicians stole a lot of money from the people and fled to America or some other western country. Years after the war ended, some Vietnamese people couldn't forget how bad the poor conditions they lived in when they were in Vietnam. South Vietnam ex-President Nguyen Cao Ky opened a business in America. His business was vandalized by some Vietnamese people as revenge for his corruption.

Years later, after I got a job in the Federal Government, when I told my veteran coworkers my story and what I heard from Vietnamese classmates. They were just so stubborn. It did not matter how I explained it to them. They just did not want to believe the Vietnamese people hated them.

America is a wealthy country. Thanks to the economic expansion and the currency exchange rate, millions of Americans travel overseas as tourists every year. In the poor nations, the people welcome the Westerners because we are the big spenders. We stay in their hotels, spending money, buying products and entertainment, giving jobs to people and money to merchants. When they have smiles on their faces, it often just means they like your money. It does not mean they like the people because we are still devils in some people's eyes.

I suggested that the American State Department should form a professional crew dedicated to foreign study. Before the American Government engages in any overseas conflict, they should recruit a study team to try to understand the mindset and situation involved with foreign countries.

The Cold War Is Over.

Here is the short story about the Cold War: After the WWII ended, there were three different kind of countries on Earth according to Mao Zedong. Mao's idea was America and Soviet Union, are the first world, which are two super powers. Other developed countries such as Western Europe, Australia, New Zealand and Japan are the second world. The poorer countries including China are called, "third world".

Here is the fact which is different than the idea about Mao's three worlds. The Soviet Union, North Korea, China, North Vietnam, Cuba, and most of Eastern Europe together formed an alliance. This was the communist world. They expanded their territory to attempt to control the world.

Against the communist world, America, most of Western Europe, Southern Europe, South Korea, Japan, and South Vietnam formed an alliance. It was called the free world.

The other nations, such as most of South America excluding Cuba, were not on either side during the Cold War.

Mao Zedong was the most powerful dictator in communist China. Because of their alliance, the Chinese had to support North Korea and North Vietnam against South Korea, South Vietnam, the USA, and the free world allies.

Today after the Cold War is over more than twenty seven years, the idea of three worlds has been changed. For today's standards, Russia is not compatible to the former Soviet Union in the past, the quality of life in today's Russia is a lower second world. In military most Russians war machines are outdated antiques left from the Cold War era. It no longer qualifies as a super power.

There is no Second Cold War presently. China replaced the former Soviet Union as another super power, next to America. China has a bigger economic power than the former Soviet Union. It is more qualified to be called a super power. The second world remains the same. The third world are developing countries. China from a third world countries becomes a first world, is an unusual successful stories just like in the past, Japan from a backward isolated country became a fantastic industrialized nation. The difference is China is much bigger and more populated than Japan.

Back to the Cold War era, there was a very big secret for the Chinese Government. Actually, the Chinese were very afraid of war. They had no choice but to get involved in those wars because they belonged to the communist allies. Back to when I was a little kid, all the major cities in China were digging bomb-proof bunkers. There were propaganda posters everywhere on the street that warned the American Imperialists would start the war to attempt to conquer China. If China did not want to be conquered by their imperialist enemies, they must support the communist brothers in fighting against them. The communist nations were actually more afraid of the free world than we were of them.

It was September 9th, 1976. Mao Zedong passed away. Shortly after, Deng Xiaoping took over. He was a foreign exchange student who used to study and work in Europe. He understood the free world that still practices capitalism. In practice, capitalism is by far superior to communism. During the Mao era, China was dirt poor. One reason is they spend too much money to prepare for wars that never happened. As a result, he wanted to make China become wealthy like the countries in free world, such as South Korea, Japan, and Taiwan. But there were some strings attached. The Chinese would get economic freedom just like the people in the free world but not in speech and politics. Eventually, these economic reforms made China become one of a super powers. I would say, during the Korean War, China was a lot like North Korea today. But today's China is much more like South Korea.

In 1979, Deng Xiaoping visited America. He signed multiple agreements with President Jimmy Carter. China has been having normal economic and trade relationships with the US ever since. This was the beginning of the end of the Cold War.

Most Americans believed the key player in ending the Cold War was Ronald Reagan. I believe, instead, it was Deng Xiaoping. Not including China and the Soviet Union, most communist nations are very small. China is the country with the largest population on Earth with nuclear weapons and long range missiles. When they suddenly pulled out of the Cold War, it became the biggest blender for the communist world. The success of China's economic reform made Eastern Europe, including the Russians, jealous and seeking to reform. As a result, between the late 1980s and early 1990s, there was a domino effect for most of the communist nations, causing their governments to collapse.

Since the late 1970's, when China began their economic reform, the trade relationship between China and South Korea increased rapidly. They had many secret agreements we may never know what they original documents said. The hostile relationship between China and South Korea ended in the middle of the 1980's. In 1992, China and South Korea recognized each other and began a normal diplomatic relationship. China became the only nation with normal diplomatic relationships with both Koreas.

On the other side, China lessened its trade with North Korea, despite them still having a normal diplomatic relationship. North Korea was never a great nation economically and they are not good agriculturally. Back to the Cold War era, because of their alliance, China and Russia were buying their industrial products and exchanged them for farm products. Everybody knows that North Korean industrial products were inferior to the same category of products that were manufactured in the free world. Since the Cold War has ended, the communist alliance no longer exists. Russia and China stopped buying industrial products from North Korea. The blunder of North Korean of economic downfall began. As a result, millions of North Korean people are starving since then.

The Chinese Government has no sympathy and is not taking care of their North Korean nephew. They see North Korea not as an ally, but as a poor beggar and neighbor. The reason they keep a diplomatic relationship is because of a political issue. I used to argue with tons of people over the Chinese Government. The Chinese Government is dominated by the communist party and there is no chance any other political party can take over. There is a lot of freedom of speech for the people, but only a handful of members of the communist party can vote. Realistically, there are many billionaire tycoon owners and foreign investors opening private businesses in China. They are not actually practicing communism, but a political party called the communist party dominates the government.

If there really was war in the Korean Peninsula, the first response would be "Is the money I deposited in South Korea safe?" Millions of starving North Korean refugees would penetrate the border and flood into China. The Chinese would definitely not want to see a second Korean War.

Without any real allies to support North Korea, the only possibility for North Korea to start the war would be if Kim Jong-Un is insane because it would be a suicide mission. Kim Jong-Un is not insane, but has a strange personality as a brutal dictator. Like many politicians, he does not want to back down or show weakness. They recognize how the communist governments of East Europe collapsed and do not want to make the same mistake. He is not elected by the people, but inherited the power from his grandfather and father. As a result, if he backed down, he would seem weak and he could be overthrown or killed by his own people.

Is Kim Jong-Un Insane

Despite the fact that North Korea had long range missiles and nuclear bombs, all of the conventional military equipment was badly outdated and with poor maintenance. I don't believe he is foolish enough to use nuclear weapons. Shortly after he press that button, he could die and millions of North Koreans who also die in vain with him. The only possibility is this brutal dictator is insane with a death wish. He wants to kill himself with millions of other people.

There is no way we could possibly send Kim Jong-Un to a psychiatrist to evaluate his mental condition. I believe he is not insane and will not start a suicidal nuclear war. I used to spend a lot of time studying psychology online. The fact is he is not an ordinary person born into a regular family. Growing up, he was a spoiled brat.

The North Korean government is a true monarchy. He inherited the dictatorship since his father Kim Jong-Il passed away, and Kim Jong-Il inherited the dictatorship from his father, Kim Il-Sung. He was born in a royal family as a prince, not an ordinary citizen. Because he was spoiled so much, he is not able to socialize with other people, causing him to have a domineering and strange personality. His order does not have to pass any legal procedure such as congress to be enforced, and there is nobody that would dare to risk his life to argue with him. You can imagine if you were born as king, you would not grow up like a regular citizen into a regular family. You would have a personality that is very strange.

One of the really bad habits for all the politicians on Earth is that they do not want to back down and say that they made a mistake unless he is ready to resign. North Korea was never a nation that enforced democracy. He only has two choices: either stay and become king, or be killed by his starving and angry people. He learned from the experience of the defeats of the ex-communist governments of Eastern Europe. He does not want to reform because he believes if he reforms, it will be another suicide mission. In front of his people and the whole world, he has to show that he always does things right and strong.

If he doesn't want to use his nuclear weapons and long-range missile, why could he spend a fortune to make these weapons? The reason is because he is a coward and is afraid the Americans will use nuclear weapons against him. This is the same thought-process that goes into buying a gun.

Imagine if someone had two hostile neighbors, both of them being bigger and stronger than you and one of the neighbors is giant also has a machine gun. His name is the USA. To defend himself against his unfriendly neighbors, he bought a pistol to protect himself. He is telling his neighbors "I will shoot you if you dare mess with me."

The major problem began at the turn of the century when George Bush was the American president. At that time, George Bush used to call Iran, Iraq, and North Korea the "Axis of Evil." Iraq never had weapons of mass destruction and did not cause any threat against America and was never involved in the September 11 attacks. Due to a mistake by the Central Intelligence Agency, the American military invaded Iraq and overthrew Saddam Hussein. This caused a violent civil war, the rise of ISIS, and made America become unpopular in the Middle East and North Korea.

After Iraq was occupied, there were no trace of weapons of mass destruction. A byproduct of this was the other two other members of the Axis of Evil, Iran and North Korea, became alert and ready for invasion. For Kim Jong-Un, his idea is America may soon invade his country. He must prepare for war. The only way to make America rethink their invasion is if he owns nuclear bombs and long range missiles. Although the weapons may never be used, it would make the Americans cancel the invasion.

But the mistake has already been made. Actually, the American Government never had a plan to invade North Korea, but the North Korean people still believe it. The Kim Jong-Un regime is a very unpopular regime that tells the people the United States is preparing to invade, causing the people to blame the Americans for their starvation and poverty. This kind of thinking is exactly like Mao Zedong during the Cold War era.

Unfortunately, the Kim Dynasty kings are worse than Mao, even though Mao is considered to be one of the most brutal dictators of the twentieth century. The other two dictators and Hitler and Stalin. One thing Mao did right was he did not want his children to inherit his power after he is dead. Shortly after Mao died, his wife, Jiang Qing, was arrested and sent to prison, where she committed suicide.

After Mao died, the Mao era was over. The Chinese Communist Party elected a more merciful leader to continue to rule China. As a result, the Chinese economic reform had begun. Deng Xiaoping and all his successors, including Xi Jinping, have ruled China since. They put economy and improving the quality of life as a major priority. They are not interested in joining in unnecessary international conflicts. As a result, North Korea is truly alone.

The Most Spoiled Brat on Earth

North Korea is a nation disconnected from the outside world. There are no telephones for civilians. The internet is reserved for only a handful of government officials. It is a typical iron curtain communist nation. The below incident is only a part of the brutal killings the outside world knows about. Nobody will ever know how many people were killed. The strange thing is that some of the executions are not done in common manners, such as hanging, firing squad, or lethal injection.

1. Hyon Yong-Chol was the Minister of the People's Armed Forces and one of the highest ranking military figures in North Korea. He was an old man and, one day, he was in a conference with Kim Jong-Un and other high-ranking military officials. It is not unusual for an older man to feel tired in a boring meeting and fall asleep. Kim Jong-Un was mad and ordered him to be executed by a quadruple anti-aircraft gun. We cannot imagine what his body looked like after the execution. The only charge was "bad attitude."

2. O Sang-hon was the deputy security minister in the Ministry of Public Security. He was executed by flamethrower.

3. A North Korean official was executed by heavy artillery.

4. Jang Song-Thaek was the Vice Chairman of the National Defense Commission of North Korea. He was Kim Jong-Un's uncle and used to be considered the second most powerful man in North Korea. Shortly after Kim Jong-Un took over, he was executed together with some of his young relatives and subordinates, including his teenage grandchildren. His aunt who was married to Jang Song-Thaek has been incarcerated since then.

5. His half-brother, Kim Jong Nam, was believed by Kim Jong-Un to be his rival despite him already having power and his half-brother already travelling to avoid him at the time. Kim Jong Nam was assassinated overseas.

6. There were several dozen people in a stadium who were mowed down by machine gun fire. The only charge those innocent people received was watching South Korean television.

7. A military official was giving his soldiers generous rations because his men and women were starving. He did not get any reward and was executed immediately.

8. An American tourist by the name of Otto Warmbier went to visit North Korea. He was arrested, sent to a hard labor camp, and was tortured repeatedly before his death. The North Korean brutal regime sent the dying young man back to America. He was not able to communicate and died shortly after. The only charge for this poor man was attempting to steal a propaganda poster.

The above stories are only a few examples of the brutal dictator's actions. Most of them will never be known. As a result, most of the outside world has reached the conclusion that Kim Jong-Un is mentally ill. A mentally ill dictator is not afraid of killing. The conclusion is he will start the war against South Korea, America, and the allies.

I used to spend a lot of leisure time studying philosophy and psychology. I believe that analysis is false. Kim Jong-Un is definitely not a nice person but he is not mentally ill. He is the most spoiled brat on Earth. North Korea is his home and he is Supreme Dictator of this nation. He can do anything he wants inside his country. It does not mean he will dare to invade any other country.

America and the free world are democratic countries. If you study history, the North Korean Kim Dynasty political system is not connected to any free nation. In 1789, the French citizens overthrew King Louis XVI. They formed a democratic government shortly after Louis XVI and his wife Marie Antoinette were executed. This incident is known as the French Revolution. After this, revolution spread to the rest of Europe and later to the rest of the world.

Kim Jong-Un is a brutal tyrant who lives like a king before the French Revolution. In the olden day imperial government, the ruler had absolute power to rule his nation. If a king did not like somebody, he could kill him and sometimes his entire family over a very small charge.

In modern society, there are different levels of spoiled. You can spoil your children, your subordinates, or your spouse. But having a spoiled child, employee, or spouse does not mean they will become dangerous outside of their home or company.

The one-child policy was a bad policy for the Chinese government and has been repealed. Because most modern Chinese families only have one child, I have seen many families spoil their children. Inside the house, they can have a very poor attitude such as yelling and screaming at their parents and constantly demanding to be bought expensive toys and clothes. But they are only spoiled inside their house. As soon as the spoiled children are outside of the house, they learn to act disciplined.

When I was a little kid, I was sitting in a classroom. My teacher asked each student what their fantasy is. Some of my classmates said they wanted to be astronauts. Some said they wanted to be movie stars. And some said they wanted to be the CEO of a company. When I told my teacher I wanted to be a king, some of my classmates laughed.

Of course, in the modern world, it is a fantasy. But there are kings who exist. Most modern nations, especially in Europe, have kings and queens with no power. The most famous one is Queen Elizabeth II. In North Korea, although they do not have the title of "King," Kim Jong-Un really is a king.

In year 2011, his father, Kim Jong-Il, suddenly died. He took office at a young age, 28. Obviously, he was a crown prince before his ascension. In the olden days, the siblings of royal imperial families fought over who would be king, sometimes becoming deadly, and rival siblings would have to die.

It was the fantasy of many men, including me. What would actually happen if you became king? You could kill anybody you don't like at any time as long as he is inside your country. You could eat whatever you want, despite the fact that your citizens are starving. You could live very well in the imperial palace, but most of your citizens would have no electrical service in their house. This is what the king of North Korea does today. But in other nations, it is a totally different story. If you have to fight other nations and you don't have the military power that can match, the obvious result is you being killed and your nation being destroyed. Of course, King Kim Jong-Un would know better than that.

Here is one example from recent history. Saddam Hussein was a brutal dictator who ruled Iraq for years. His brutal actions against humanity were pretty similar to the actions of Kim Jung-un today. The difference is Iraq had oil and money. They were able to use their oil and cash in exchange for weapons while the Kim Dynasty cannot. There was a small nation, Kuwait that used to belong to Iraq. As soon as Saddam Hussein invaded Kuwait, America and the International Task Force formed an alliance against Iraq. The Iraqi troops suffered large casualties and retreated from Kuwait. Kim Jong-Un is brutal but not stupid or insane. He knew what brought an end to Saddam Hussein's tyranny and will not make the same mistakes.

A Mad Man Vs A Mad Woman

Here is a mystery of human behavior. Most people can be either Dr. Jekyll or Mr. Hyde. An ancient Chinese philosopher, Han Fei, is one of the most influential philosophers and politicians in Chinese history next to Confucius and Mencius. He believed society needs law and order to control people's behavior. If there is no law, everyone could become criminals.

Xun Zhi is another famous Chinese philosopher. He believed all human beings are born imperfect and evil and that education is the only way to make human beings civilized. When a person is born greedy, jealous, violent, perverse, and sadistic, it's natural.

In modern times, when America overthrew Saddam Hussein, some Iraqi territories were left as lawless anarchies. As a result, chaos occurred. There was excessive violence between people fighting including suicide bombings with kill dozens and sometime hundreds of people in each attack. The blood bath along with the rise of ISIS.

Another example, in East Asia, the laws against illegal drugs such as cocaine and heroin were very strict. Most countries in East Asia had the death penalty for drug dealers. America, Canada, and Western Europe have very large numbers of people abusing drugs. The death toll among drug users in America has been increasing consistently. The problem is with the lawmakers in western society are too tolerant. The penalty for drug dealers is minimal in comparison to the rest of the world. The looser the laws, the more crime.

What would happen if you became the supreme dictator of a nation? You would be above the law. You could do whatever you want. For most people, this is only a daydream.

In recent Chinese history, the longest serving and the most unpopular dictator is not Mao Zedong but Empress Dowager Cixi (1835 to 1908). She ruled China from 1861 to 1908. There have been an enormous amount of movies and TV series and in theatres. One of the most famous actresses to play her is Liu Xiaoqing.

In all the Chinese people mind, because of the influence of modern movies and books, she is regarded as the most brutal dictator in recent Chinese history.

Below were some famous incidents:

In 1861, she murdered several government officials to win her dictatorship.

She stole the military budget to build the imperial palace. As a result, in 1894, the Chinese army tried to save Korea from Japanese invaders and the war was defeated.

In 1898, she murdered six politicians and imprisoned the puppet emperor Guangxu to increase her power.

In 1900, she ordered the Boxer Rebellion to fight against the foreigners in China, leading to the country being attacked by Eight-Nation Alliance. China was defeated and forced to pay an enormous amounts in compensation to foreign countries.

In her personal life, she was considered to be a madwoman. Famous incidents:

Consort Zhen was the puppet emperor Guangxu's most beloved concubine. One day, she dressed as a man and tried to play a joke on the emperor. When Empress Cixi saw Consort Zhen dressed as a man, she became furious and ordered her to be stripped naked, destroy the clothes she wears and beaten. Because her clothes were destroyed, she had to walk back to her room naked.

In 1894, in a separate incident, Consort Zhen was accused of taking a bribe. The empress asked "Did you take a bribe?" She replied "I was just following in your footsteps." Cixi was furious and ordered Consort Zhen to be stripped naked and beaten. She was three months pregnant at the time. As a result, she had a miscarriage. This was probably the worst punishment a royal consort has ever been dealt aside from the death penalty.

Consort Zhen was believed to be the most beautiful woman in the Forbidden City at the time. In 1900, just before the Eight Nation Alliance conquered Beijing, Cixi worried that the beautiful consort would be raped by the foreign enemies. She was murdered by the empress by thrown into a well. Jealous, destructive, and sadistic are natural imperfect qualities in people.

Empress Cixi was a sadistic madwoman. Unlike Kim Jong-Un, she didn't kill a lot of people but she did, however, punish a lot of people. When there was a little disagreement between her and her royal servants, she would order the servants she did not like to be stripped naked and beaten. Most of them were young women or girls. Some psychologists believed this was a fetish for her. Although she wasn't a lesbian. Those incidents were repeatedly shown in popular films. You may be disappointed if you watch these films on YouTube because, in China, the films were censored.

She liked to gamble and she liked to cheat. She also liked to take bribes and steal. People asked, "What does she need so much money for?" Greed is a natural and imperfect quality in people. Her stolen items which included some priceless national treasure. By the time before her death, she ordered to build an enormous tomb. The treasures she stole she took to the grave.

She died in 1908. Twenty years later, a warlord, General Sun Dian Ying blew up the door of the tomb with dynamite and stole all the treasure she took to the grave, including the fancy coat she was entombed in and let her incorruptible corpse lay on the floor naked. The warlord's soldiers humiliate her naked corpse. The general public made fun of her. They said Cixi tried to steal everything and she was left with nothing.

When the last emperor, Pu Yi, heard the news, he suffered a panic attack and fainted. General Sun Dian Ying not only robbed the tomb of Cixi. He also robbed the tomb of famous emperor Qianlong. At the time, the penalty for the theft of an imperial tomb was death. But General Sun Dian Ying was never punished. One reason was because Cixi was the most unpopular Empress in Chinese history. Anyone who robbed her tomb and humiliated her corpse would be considered a hero.

Another reason General Sun was not punished is because the Nationalist Government in China was very corrupt. He bribed the high-ranking government officials, including President Chiang Kai-shek and his wife Soong Mei-ling, with some of the treasure from Cixi's tomb.

In a previous section, I wrote how the American government was mistakenly helping some corrupt foreign governments, such as the Chinese Nationalist government and South Vietnam. As a result, a lot of foreigners, including anti-American rebels like the Vietcong, fought against the American troops.

There were a lot of rumors that she had many lovers. When her husband Emperor Xian Feng passed away, she was only 26. What would she do for the rest of her life? She had been looking for lovers since her husband's death. Perversion is one of the most natural human qualities and it exists in almost everyone. Because China is a male-dominated society, if she were a man, she could have simply taken on many wives. But she could not have taken on many spouses as a woman.

One of Cixi's lovers was Sir Edmund Backhouse. He published a book China Under the Empress Dowager. His book contained erotic stories about the empress. Unlike Donald Trump and Bill Clinton, the famous American presidents, she wants more physical sex. Normally, an old lady is not having the sex drive as strong as a man. Some people don't believe the stories are true. Although the stories may have been exaggerated, I studied philosophy for decades and I believe the statements could be true.

America is a democratic country. The president is not immune from complaints or lawsuits. In imperial China the empress is immune from any charges and she is above the law, as a result she could be more aggressive than Donald Trump and Bill Clinton.

Imagine if you live in Russia back to the Tsars era, one day the Empress of Russia, Catherine the great sent an envoy to your house, the envoy said "the Empress order you go to meet her in her bedroom privately". What is your choice? Have sex with her or die? Some men get both.

Besides heightened sexuality one of the reasons was for revenge. Nineteenth Century Imperial China was one of the most chauvinistic societies on Earth. Men can have many wives, especially the emperors. Any woman despite even the nobility or the ultra-rich can only have one husband. There is very clear gender role. If a woman has a lover or inappropriate relationship with other man, not just the law works against it, but the culture is against it.

Suddenly, a woman becomes the Supreme Dictator Even the emperor is a position under her. What would she like to do? Having many lovers at the same time is a rebellious act against the traditional culture. In the past the Tang Dynasty Empress Wu Zetian (624-705 AD) did the same thing. As soon as she become the supreme dictator of the country, she had multiple lovers at the same time as a rebellious act against a chauvinist culture.

She was the supreme ruler of the nation. She lived above the law and there was no one to limit her power. Because she was a woman living in a very chauvinistic society, she was highly criticized. She was actually not any worse than most of China's male emperors. The defeat of the Chinese military was not her responsibility since she was not in charge of it.

Eventually, big trouble arrived. During the Cixi Era, China was invaded by the foreign imperialists. The corrupted Qing Dynasty lost every wars that was against the invasions. The Qing Government being forced by the invaders sign multiple unfair treaties. The majority of Chinese people were furious about the nation being over ruled by other nations. The Chinese people formed an organization named Boxers to against the imperialist invaders.

The Boxers didn't carry modern weapons. They used swords, spears, and bows and arrows just like the medieval armies to fight the foreign armies with guns and cannons. The empress was ignorant in military and believed the Boxer Rebellion could defeat the foreign armies with medieval weaponry that was several hundreds of years behind technology.

She ordered the Boxers attack the foreigners in Beijing and attempt to capture compounds in which foreign embassies were located with their medieval era weapons. The foreign embassies immediately telegraphed their own country and send troops into China to save them. Eight nations, America, Russia, Great Britain, Germany, France, Austria, Italy and Japan quickly formed an Eight Nation Alliance and deployed to China to save their people and embassy.

Of course, anyone could imagine what the result was. The Boxers were never able to seize the compounds and embassies. Cixi supported the Boxer rebellion was defeated by the Eight Nation Alliance. The Eight Nation Alliance conquered Beijing. Cixi dressed as a female farmer, escaped from the imperial palace, and fled.

The corrupted Qing Government were forced to sign the biggest unfair treaty in history with Eight Nations Alliance named Boxer Protocol. China not just have to compensate an enormous amount of money. The Chinese lost a lot of legal and economic rights to foreign nations.

Kim Jong-Un is a supreme ruler with no limit to his power, much like Cixi. The North Korean military has the weaponry generations behind modern day standards, just like the Boxer Rebellion did trying to fight the foreigners with their inferior weapons. If history repeats itself and Kim Jong-Un dares to conflict with other nations, as soon as they launch the attack, other nations will join forces against North Korea, occupy the capital, and expel or kill him.

The Different Political Culture

The political idea for every nation is like a culture or religion. This is set in stone for generations. North America and Western Europe is considered the free world. People living in the free world don't understand other countries political system. Just like the Christians may not understand Buddhism or Confucianism or other popular beliefs in Asia. The people of other parts of the world don't recognize Christianity.

Here are some political nonsense pertaining to free world's politics. The freedom to vote, freedom of religion, freedom of press and speech, freedom to bear arms, and the idea of all men created equal regardless of racial and sexual orientation are not popular nor are recognized in different worldly regions, even pertaining to some close American allies.

America and Western Europe are the birthplace of democracy. This not only pertains to people can enjoy freedoms and equal rights they also have the economic freedom the people can create their own business and create wealth. The successful path of capitalism attracts the people from all over the world to immigrate to the West. Including the people who come from the region which is hostile and opposes the West. Mostly it is based on wealth and quality of life they want to achieve. In most cases it may have nothing to do with gaining equal rights or freedom.

An example is that Japan is one of America's closest allies. In the eyes of the general public in Japan they don't believe in freedom of religion, nor right to bear arms. They don't believe the people's race and sex are inherently equal. There are some unwritten laws, prohibited to make fun or insult the emperor of Japan. Unlike in the western societies making fun of famous figures such as the Queen of England and the members of the royal family.

Japan, North and South Korea, Taiwan and most of the part of China have something similar. The permanent citizen who lives in those countries are the same color. They do not have a minority population in both Koreas. Japan has very few immigrants. China and Taiwan has the overwhelmingly Han ethnic majority. 92 percent of Chinese are Han ethnic. 95 percent of the Taiwanese are Han ethnic. In both places most of the non-ethnic majority are the same color of people. To gain popularity and friends like job searching some non-Han Chinese would hide and not mention their ethnic background. Some people simply convert to be Han.

The setup of the societies on Eastern Asia is different from North America and Western Europe. If a western politician goes to eastern Asia and talks about freedom of religion, the equal rights of women and men, and minority rights, would be unpopular because western values clash with those of the East.

Excluding some rural and remote part of China such as Xinjiang. There were few or no people following Islam. The vast majority people in China has a strong sense of Islamophobia. To avoid persecution some minorities was originally Muslims. Later they converted out to Atheists and modified their dress codes. If there is politicians asking Han ethnic people in Taiwan to stop the discrimination against the Muslim minority they would be fiercely rejected. It would be the same as asking an individual to change the culture.

When I attended high school in Hong Kong, I wrote a book report talking about religion. When I went to a bookstore and found an anti-Islamic book. It is the most anti-Islamic book I ever see. If this book was translated to English and published in America it would be hate-speech. It seemed like there must be an unwritten rule concerning Islamic bans.

Japan has a capitalist economic system identical to the West. But the culture differs. Japanese store or restaurant owners maintains the right to expel unwanted customers with no specific reason. As an example somebody wearing Islamic dress code can be expelled from the premises. Or a restaurant can refuse services to foreign born individual. If the same situation occurred in the west, the owner would be punished.

Not including laws written by politicians, there are certain unwritten expectations for different cultures. When I was in school my teacher told me that he had a friend living in Japan, he planned to publish a book talking about the Japanese culture springing from ancient Chinese culture. The Japanese people were the descendants from China, including the Emperor of Japan. My teacher told him don't publish this book in Japan. The Japanese people would have him assassinated. If a similar book was published in North America or Europe there would be no backlash against him.

In the Middle East the situation is far worse. There is no such thing as separation of church and state. In some strong held Muslim nations not obeying Islamic rules could be a capital crime punished by death. Unlike the Queen of England, some Islamic countries the kings have political power. Homosexuality is punished by death. There is no freedom of speech or freedom of press. Women have to obey Islamic dress code. Some Islamic nations prohibit women to drive a car. The people born and grow up in extreme Islamic nations may consider the lifestyle and political ideas such as freedom and equality are unacceptable by their standards.

Freedom, Rights and democracy are a forms of political beliefs in Western society. Like somebody believing Christianity if you go to a foreign country dominated by other religions, Christianity is being persecuted in many countries, sometimes violently including imprisonment and execution.

The Wrong Path to Reach Democracy

A nation moving from a traditional monarchy to a true democracy, like America or Western Europe is a bumpy road. It could take as much as a century to make a nation become a great democracy power. Nazi Germany is the most famous example of a defective democracy.

The defeat of WWI forced the last Kaiser of the German Emperor Wilhelm II to lose his power and be exiled. The sudden defeat of the German Empire made Germany have no other choice but to become a democracy. The Weimar Republic was constructed in such a hurry, the German people were not ready to make the nation become a true democracy. As a result, shortly after the Weimar Republic form, the government was hijacked by Adolf Hitler and put all of Europe in turmoil.

The path to a true democracy in the US was tough too. In the beginning, not every American had the right vote. For example, people of color and women were excluded. Even after Abraham Lincoln freed the slaves and the 19th amendment, ratified in 1920, allowed women to vote, women and minorities still did not fully have equal rights, until the Civil Rights Era.

Before the Civil Rights Era, there was a lot of prejudice and inequality. It became a part of the culture. It took 200 years for the Americans to create the greatest free nation.

The road for the French from an autocratic monarchy to a true democracy was a rough ride. In the late 18th century, imperial France was a corrupt monarchy government. King Louis XVI was an unfit ruler. Most of the French people were living in poverty. They put their anger towards Louis XVI and his government. As a result, he was overthrown and beheaded.

Unfortunately, the French people were not prepared for democracy. After the French Revolution, because people were not trained and did not understand the meaning of democracy, the first democratic government formed in Europe was a failure. The people did not understand how to vote, but they used violence against their political rivals. It put this nation in a terrible bloodshed. Millions of people, including some famous politicians, were killed. The other European nations formed allies and tried to extinguish the revolutionary movement. Later, in 1799, the democracy was hijacked by the famous general Napoleon Bonaparte.

After Napoleon took over the government, he did not like democracy as well as most French people who don't what having a democracy is. In 1804. Napoleon overthrew the democratic government and crowned himself as the Emperor was France. The chaos continued. He could be compared to Hitler while living a century earlier. There used to be a lot of people who argued that the Napoleonic War should have been called WWI, WWI should be called WWII, and WWII should be called WWIII.

After decades of bloodshed, Napoleon was finally defeated and was exiled. The allies brought Louis XVIII to rule France and restore the monarchy. But next year, Napoleon came back to France, kicked out the king, and declared himself as the Emperor of France again. Finally, he was defeated in the Battle of Waterloo in 1815. He was exiled again to Saint Helena until he died in 1822. The allies brought back King Louis XVIII to rule France and restore the monarchy again.

Upon King Louis XVIII's death, his brother ascended to the throne in 1824, as King Charles X. In 1830, Charles X was deposed and replaced by King Louis Philippe. French people wanted to be free and did not like the monarchy. The bloodshed continued. Eventually, the Revolution of 1848, the people got rid of the French monarchy and restarted the republic. It was called the French Second Republic.

The story repeated. The second republic was short lived. Napoleon III was like Napoleon Bonaparte reincarnated. In 1848, he became the French president, four years later, he hijacked the government and became the Emperor of France. He put his nation to war against other European nations, destroyed the republic, and formed the last imperial government.

One of the differences between Napoleon I and Napoleon III is Napoleon III did not have the military expertise like his uncle did. He was much more willing to give up the fight against his enemies. In 1870, he surrendered to the Prussians together with over 100,000 soldiers which is one of the biggest blunders in French military history before they surrendered to Germany in WWII. After his defeat, France became a democracy again.

People used to believe you can force other nations from either a monarchy or dictatorship to become a democratic government. This would not only not work, but create chaos. Unfortunately, people would not learn from this mistake. Democracy takes people being educated and trained to understand it. The process takes generations of people. North Korea is not ready for this.

If Kim Jong-Un was suddenly assassinated or overthrown, it would create a non-stop civil war over who would control the nation, just like after Saddam Hussein was overthrown. Even today, there is ongoing violence including suicide bombing, which is quite often. The better way to handle the situation in North Korea would be to isolate them and ignore them.

The Differences between China and North Korea

The country with a history most similar to China is Korea. In the past, China was almost identical to North Korea in politics, culture, and economic standings. After the economic reform, China is almost identical to South Korea in culture and economic standings, although there are differences in politics.

China and Korea have a history of imperial governments, dynasties, and rulers who've dominated their countries for generations. In the previous section, we spoke about there always being a bumpy road from overthrowing an imperial government to becoming a democracy. The path may be very different. Although China is not a complete democracy, the "quality of life" is much better than a lot of other communist or ex-communist countries. At least the people now can live a lot better than they used to. But North Korea, however, has remained an absolute monarchy with its people living under poor conditions and they are not going to become a democracy anytime soon. Below is a recent history of both China and North Korea.

Qing Dynasty (1644 to 1912) is the last dynasty in China. After the defect of the Opium War in 1841, the imperialist invaders from Europe and Japan invaded China continuously, building colonies and making the Qing Government sign unfair treaties, as well as China losing all of their protectorates, such as Korea and Vietnam. As a result, the anger between the general public to blaming the imperial government.

Since the defect of the Opium War, the corrupted Qing Dynasty lost every war against foreign invaders. Some politicians come up with a new idea to create and privatize the military system. This military system is called the Beiyang Army.

The soldiers in this army don't directly respond to the central government. The commander generals set their own rules and standards. Their goals and ambitions was to demolish the old and tear it down and rebuild the entire defense system. The major problem is those generals are military men, they were never educated in politics. They don't understand what is rights, freedom and democracy. When the Imperial Qing Dynasty exists they serve the imperial government. What would happen is suddenly the imperial government was overthrown. They believe who has guns and armies who could ascend to the next ruler.

In 1911, the revolution led by Sun Yat-Sen started the Xinhai Revolution. A few months later, the Beiyang Army changed sides together with the revolutionaries to oppose the imperial government. The last Emperor of China resigned, and they formed a new nation named the Republic of China.

Unfortunately, the situation of the Chinese Revolution is pretty similar to the French Revolution and runs parallel. Most of the Chinese people are not educated and not ready for democracy. The central government is not powerful enough to stabilize the nation. Shortly after, Sun Yat-Sen resigned as president, and the next president was a famous Beiyang Army warlord Yuan Shikai.

Yuan Shikai, after becoming the president, had exactly the same thought as Napoleon. He doesn't respect the democratic government, and the people were not ready for democracy. Their minds were still living in traditional imperial era. In 1916, he declared himself the Emperor of China and changed the nation from the Republic of China to the Empire of China. Fortunately, he did not live very long. He died of natural causes on the same year.

After the death Yuan Shikai, the central government was hijacked by warlords. They had the president, congress, and senators, but this government did not get the respect from the other warlords who controlled each provinces through the country. They were not able to make a united government, but they fought each other. In 1917, a warlord named Zhang Xun restored the imperial government and made the last emperor, Pu Yi, become the emperor again. It did not last long. Shortly after, other warlords overthrew the imperial government again and rebuilt the Republic.

Although the republican government was restored, the damage was already done. The central government could only control a small territory and the warlords ruled each province. Since the people were very disappointed in the revolution and the worthless republican government, a group of people founded a new political party in 1921, which was the Chinese Communist Party. In the future the reason China became communist it was because the democracy was defeated. The Chinese people were not ready for these changes and democratic rule.

After decades of civil war, eventually, the republican government which was hijacked by warlords was overthrown and replaced by the Chinese Nationalists. One of the most famous and longest serving presidents is Chiang Kai-Shek. Unfortunately, the Nationalist Government was not any better at handling the interior problems better than the Qing Dynasty Government or the warlords' Beiyang Governments. They were just as corrupt as the

South Vietnamese Government in the Vietnam War era. There were people disappointed with the Nationalist Government and turned their hope to the communists.

In 1937, the Japanese started a full scale war against China. The Nationalist Army was so corrupt, half of the nation was conquered by the Japanese invaders. Not until 1945 did the Japanese surrender. The Nationalist Government was deeply weakened.

When the war was almost over, the Russian Red Army crossed the border and took over Manchuria and North Korea. After the Japanese surrendered, under the help by the Russian Red Army, the Chinese Communists secured the Japanese weapons left in Manchuria and other part of China. Although before WWII finished the communist China had a big army, their weaponry was poor. They seized the weaponry from the Japanese army become a major turning point between the communist against the nationalists. In 1949 the communists defeated the nationalists and took over China. Throughout history a corrupt government deals with an army that can't fight. The Chinese Communist army defected the Chinese Nationalist army just like the North Vietnamese Communist army defeated the Southern Vietnamese Government army.

The Chinese people were not ready for communism either, and neither was the Communist Party ready for Mao. Chairman Mao Zedong did not have the mind of a true communist. Secretly, he still had a lot of ideas believing himself as a supreme ruler, just like an emperor. The reason the Chinese Communist Government during the Mao era was so highly controlled and dominated by Mao was because he was more like an emperor during the new era than an elected government official.

Fortunately, during the last few years of Mao's life, he recognized it would be a bad idea to have his children inherit his power. He chose a younger and much less powerful man, Hua Guofeng to be the next dictator. As a result, after he died in 1976, the next dictator Hua Guofeng lacking political support. He was not able to control the nation and the government was taken over by Deng Xiaoping in 1977. This was a major turning point of China.

When Deng Xiaoping was young, he was a foreign exchange student. He eye-witnessed the superiority of capitalism in Western Europe. In 1979, China and America officially established a normal trade and diplomatic relationship. In the same year he visited America. During the American visit, He signed several agreements with President Jimmy Carter. He witnessed the superior industrial power America had and the superior quality of life American people had. As a result, he made an important decision to reform the economy and made China accept foreign investments and allowed people to make their own businesses. Although this was not a political reform, only an economic reform. After the death of Deng Xiaoping in 1997, his successors continued to reform and make China almost like other capitalistic countries. I used to argue with people that **China is a capitalist nation with a Communist Party**.

Most of the people outside China do not understand how the Chinese Government today was formed. There is a closed-door election inside the Communist Party. Unlike Mao Zedong, he was elected by the Chinese Communist Party in 1935. He hijacked the government shortly afterwards. Not until he died 41 years later as a supreme dictator. Today, there is no supreme dictator in the Chinese Government. The Chinese president is Xi Jinping. He cannot continue his rule and must be reelected after a five-year term.

The Korean history is almost identical to the Chinese with a monarchy government. They were taken over by the Japanese invaders. The problem about why the nation is still under absolute monarchy rule is because the creation of the nation was a historical mistake made by President Franklin Roosevelt during the Yalta Conference in 1945. During the Yalta Conference, President Roosevelt asked Stalin three months after the Nazi surrendered to the allies, the Russian declared war on Japan and invaded North Korea and Manchuria.

Stalin fulfilled his promise. After the Nazi surrendered, three months later, Russia invaded North Korea and Manchuria. The Russian troops faced very little resistance, because the Japanese were forced to surrender after the atom bombs were dropped. The Red Army conquered Manchuria and North Korea easily. The Russians seized the weapons the Japanese left and gave it to the communists in both countries. Not only was this a great help in helping the Chinese Communists beat the Nationalists in the Chinese Civil War, but also helped to create North Korea.

The major problem is in North Korea, before the communists arrived, the people were not trained to accept the modern political idea. Both communism and democracy were too new for them, but the people remembered, before they were conquered by the Japanese, it was an Imperial Korean Government. As a result, the North Korean Communist Government was worse than other communist governments. The Chinese Communist Government and the East European Communist governments have scheduled in party elections but the North Korean election is false. The communist governments in China and Eastern Europe had a little bit of time to prepare for the communist rule before they were taken over by communists, but not North Korea. The communists just suddenly arrived kicked out the Japanese invader and forced them to become communist.

Before WWII ended, the Chinese Communist Party was already a powerful political party. They had a powerful army, controlled large amounts of rural areas in China, and were supported by a certain number of people. The North Korea communists had a different story. Although there was a communist party in Korea during the Japanese occupation, the communists were very weak and had little support. Just before the Japanese surrendered, the Red Army unexpectedly took over the region and forced the people in that region to accept communism. In fact, the people who lived in the region were not ready for it.

In North Korea, the dictatorship is inherited through the generations. It is an absolute monarchy government, and the creation of North Korea is a historical mistake. The election for North Korea is nonsense. There is no way in a democratic government for the leader to have 100 percent of the votes. Because there is only one candidate on the ballot, and every citizen is afraid to vote no.

The Kim Dynasty officials eye-witnessed between the late 1980's to the early 1990's the domino effect of the fall of the communist governments in Eastern Europe. Kim Jong-Un is afraid if he reforms his country, the people will execute him like Louis XVI. There is no way to expect any miracle to happen for a bright future for North Korea.

There have been three generations of the North Korean dictatorship. Kim Il-Sung was the first dictator. After his death, his son Kim Jong-Il took over. After Kim Jong-Il died, Kim Jong-Un took over. Such a system is typical Monarchy government. The biggest problem stemming from a monarchy government is the incoming ruler who inherited the power from his father and/or older relatives. It does not matter his personal qualities or not. Each generation descended into further and further abuse. This situation is exactly like the Imperial French government before the French Revolution, but they are much worse.

Louis the XIV (1638 to 1715) is longest serving king and one of the greatest rulers in Frances history. He ruled a golden era of Imperial France. He made France become one of the most powerful nations in Europe. After he passed, his decedent was crowned as Louis XV (1710 to 1774). He does not have the capacity to rule as well as Louis XIV. The government fell to corruption. This planted the seeds for the French Revolution.

After Louis XV passed away, the big trouble arrived. King Louis XVI (1754 to 1793) was too slow to keep up with the demands that the throne placed on him. The nobility and the church were paying almost no tax, and the majority lower class people were starving. The blame was placed on the King and his Queen Marie Antoinette, the noblemen, and the church.

As a result the French Revolution began. The King, the Queen and a lot of government officials plus the church officials were beheaded.

In the Kim Dynasty, the founder, Kim Il-Sung, was not as capable as Louis XIV. If it were not because the Russian Red Army taking over North Korea and giving the land to him, there would never be a Kim Dynasty. There is no such thing as a golden era in North Korea since the communists took over. During the 1970's, the quality of life in North Korea was approximately similar to China at the same time. Since the late 1970's, the Chinese have been reforming the economy and the North Koreans were never able to keep pace.

As soon as Kim Il-Sung passed away, the nation was taken over by his son, who had less capabilities in politics, and the entire nation deteriorated. The quality of life during the Kim Jong-Il era sharply declined. Between 1994-1998, there was a major food shortage which caused a mass starvation. Nobody would ever know how many people starved because of the iron curtain, but it was approximately ten percent of the population who starved to death. This situation is much worse than the Chinese Great Leap Forward. Between 1959 to 1962, roughly 5 percent of people in China starved to death. After 1962, we no longer hear about major crises that make people starve to death in China anymore, but in North Korea, the problem continues. Until recently, it still had people who died from malnutrition.

In 2011, Kim Jong-Il passed away. The bigger trouble arrived. The Kim Dynasty crowned an inexperienced young prince named Kim Jong-Un, who was less than 30 years old at the time, to be king. Before the young king took over, North Korea was already facing big economic troubles. He ignored the advice of his only close ally, the Chinese Government officials, not to develop nuclear weapons and long-range missiles. As a result, it caused international sanctions. In the United Nations, both Russia and China supported the sanctions, although the Chinese never made the sanctions very tight because they are afraid the North Korean regime may collapse or become very unstable, thus damaging the Chinese international reputation.

Somebody may think "Why is it that the North Korean people do not overthrow their tyrant king?" Back to before the French Revolution, the French people had limited freedom of speech and freedom of press. Some philosophers such as Voltaire, Jean-Jacques Rousseau, and Charles Louis de Secondat published books and made speeches against the French Monarchy. This could not happen in North Korea.

What May Happen if Kim Jong-Un is Assassinated

If they are not able to have the North Korean people overthrow the Kim Dynasty, what would happen if Kim Jong-Un was assassinated? The assassination could be committed by his own people or a foreign government, such as the American Navy Seals or CIA. I used to see some fictional articles about people planning to assassinate Kim Jong-Un with a long-range high-powered sniper rifle, unmanned drones, air dropped smart bombs, cruise missiles, or even high-tech weapons such as lasers. Those are all make-believe, fictional stories. I believe if he were to be assassinated, the Kim Dynasty would just have one of the Kim's relatives to take over and become the new king. It may not change the base of the monarchy government.

During the Russian Communist Revolution, the last Tsar of Russia, Nicholas II, was overthrown. His whole family, including his wife and five children, were all killed. In about the same time, the Russian Communists kill a lot of Tsars' close relatives. The main reason was because during the beginning of the revolution, the communist officials believed if they did not kill of everybody who is capable of being the next Tsar, if the revolution is defeated and the communists lose the war, they will bring back a new Tsar to continue to monarchy rule. Today is the 21st century and the people are more humane. It is highly unlikely they will kill off the entire Kim family like the Russian Communists did a hundred years ago.

To overthrow a dynasty, it is a more difficult operation than just killing a dictator. Before Hitler committed suicide in April 30, 1945, nobody knew who would take charge of the Third Reich after Hitler died. Since everybody understood it, nobody could save the Third Reich. A week later, Hitler's successor, Karl Donitz, surrendered to the Allies. If you have to get rid of the Kim Dynasty, assassinating the dictator is not a solution. As soon as he died one of Kim's relatives will become the next king. They must send in ground troops to occupy the entire nation, like what the Allies did to Nazi Germany. The price could be very high, including materiel and casualties.

In modern warfare, to defeat an invader and make them retreat back to their own nation like the First Gulf War in 1991, when Iraq was defeated and retreated from Kuwait was an easy operation. If North Korea dares to invade South Korea, unless Kim Jong-Un is crazy enough to use his nuclear weapons, it would cause a catastrophic reprisal. The South Korean military could defeat the North Koreans easily because their weapons systems are generations more advanced and the North Korean soldiers are starving. Without the Americans and other countries involvement, the South could push them back across the border to take over North Korea and end the Kim Dynasty. I believe Kim Jong-Un is not as crazy as we though he might be. This is why he makes a lot of threats, but never takes action; because we know what would happen if South Korea takes the first shot and crosses the border.

The Americans have a different philosophy about military than the communist regimes. If a country is ruled by a communist regime or if a government is ruled by a dictator, the life of a soldier or a civilian is meaningless to the dictators. During the Korean and Vietnam Wars, the Americans had much fewer causalities than their communist enemies. The difference is the life of an American soldier or US citizen counts as more important for the politicians. Unlike Hitler, Mao or Stalin, for whom a person's life means nothing. What they see is winning the wars they fight.

After the Allies overthrew Saddam Hussein, Iraq was occupied. The insurgents launched daily attacks against the Americans and their allies. In fact, the casualties for American soldiers in Iraq was significantly lower than in Vietnam. The difference is the politicians and the American people do not have the will to stay in Iraq and see us lose our lives. Despite the war deaths for the Americans in the second Gulf War being less than a tenth of the Vietnam War, Shortly after Obama was elected, the American troops retreated from Iraq, and left the chaos behind, such as the non-stop civil war and ISIS expansion.

The North Korean people were brainwashed for several decades to hate Americans. If war began, it would repeat the same high casualties just like in the Korea and Vietnam War. The difference is after several decades, the American culture changed. Back to WWII, the Americans won the war against the Japanese and the Nazis, at the price of 400,000 military deaths. The more modern it is, the less the Americans are worried about the lives of American soldiers. If the Americans had the same politicians control congress as during WWII who were so afraid of military deaths, the Nazis would take over Europe and the Japanese would take over Asia. To win or lose a war is not about the military itself. It is about if the politicians have the courage to win the war. Some people say America never lost the Vietnam War. It was the politicians who made America retreat without winning the war. I suggest, if the American politicians and the American people are so afraid of war casualties, the US Government should form a contracted, militarized organization, like the French Foreign Legion or Gurkha, to fight for America.

Cultural Conflict between Nations

There are many different cultures on Earth. A lot of people in the free world do not understand the cultures in some other countries and, in some other countries, the people don't understand the culture of the free world. Politicians and military personnel are just like the majority of people. They don't understand other people's cultures.

Here is a fact: In a lot of other countries, there is no freedom of religion. Church and state are not separate. They are one. In some other countries, the dictators is not just the lord, but God. Some other countries constantly make propaganda to attack western culture. **Living like a westerner or looking like one is considered a crime**. It would be foolish for a westerner to believe he would be welcome everywhere on earth and that everyone on earth likes freedom.

Somethings you can see without words. In some predominately Muslim countries, how do the diplomats dress? How does Kim Jong-Un dress? During the Cold War era, how would a diplomat from East Asia, such as from China or North Vietnam, dress? They did not wear suits and ties like westerners. Since the Cold War ended, the Chinese people changed their dress code. Today, they dress like westerners because they want to keep a good relationship with the Western World and accept some of the Western culture.

America is a beautiful, free country. She has freedom of religion, press, speech, etc. People must appreciate and understand the value of freedom and how to use it. In some other cultures, some people are very stubborn. They will consider free speech, freedom of religion, and freedom of press as crimes because they were brainwashed by propaganda for generations.

There is no chance you can "endorse freedom" as George Bush says because people in Iraq do not appreciate freedom. The 2003 Second Gulf War incited chaos and bloodshed after Saddam Hussein was overthrown. This proves you cannot force a culture ruled by a dictator for a long time to appreciate freedom. In the news, before the American soldiers retreated from Iraq, there were daily attacks against Americans, military, and civilians. Some people just will not get it. How can you believe Iraqi people will love Americans when Americans will just shoot them from every direction?

Thanks to an economic miracle, America is one of the wealthiest countries on Earth. Although some countries have a higher GDP per capita, those countries are all very small, such as Norway, Luxembourg, and Switzerland. America is the wealthiest large-sized country on Earth.

Decades ago, I was told there was almost no chance I could go to college in Hong Kong. I immigrated to America, attended college, got a job, and made a family. When I read the news, for the majority of people in Hong Kong, their living conditions are very poor. Most of the people are living in very small condominiums, which are described as shoebox apartments. They are very expensive, yet they are small apartments, each the size of a garage. They sell for approximately 1 million USD. The living space is so crammed, and air pollution and noise are big problems. Most people cannot afford to buy even a small apartment, and they have to pay a lot of money for their rent. Some lower income people have cannot afford to rent an apartment for their own. They have to share their apartments with roommates.

Education is a disaster in Hong Kong. I remember, when I graduated elementary school in 1976, some of my classmates told me they are not planning to attend middle school. They planned only on working in a factory or a restaurant. Fortunately, my family had enough money for me to go to middle school. Just before I graduated high school, some people, including my teacher, told me that, if I stayed in Hong Kong, I would most likely not be accepted into college because there are only three colleges there. As a result, I went to America. Years later, during my mom's birthday party, some of my relatives asked me what kind of job I'm doing now. I said I'm an engineer. Everyone at the party was surprised. Most of my relatives don't even have a high school diploma.

I live in a five-bedroom house in America. My garage is the size of a regular mid-sized apartment in Hong Kong. Very few people in Hong Kong own cars because a parking space is worth a fortune. I own two cars. I can simply leave my cars in the garage or in the driveway. I live like an ultra-rich person in Hong Kong. **I greatly appreciate the economic success in America and I love America.**

The American politicians either do not understand or play dumb. When foreign immigrants move into America, it is extremely rare for them to be looking for freedom. People who love America and immigrate looking for freedom is a fairy tale for American politicians. The majority of people who move to America are looking for education, higher paying jobs, and better living conditions. They do not necessarily love American culture or anything else.

There are a lot of people who immigrate to America and live here for a long time who do not necessarily love this country, just the materials she provides. As an example, a lot of doctors and pharmacists are Indian. I used to tell my kids "If you want to get rich, try to become a doctor." Doctors in America make a lot of money. If you know how much doctors make in India, you would not be surprised how many doctors will leave India and come to America. It does not mean doctors in India love America or are looking for freedom, since India is a free country. The doctors go to America because they earn much higher pay and there are better living conditions.

It can be dangerous for non-screened immigrants to enter America because the people who hate America, such as foreign terrorists, could come into America and commit terrorist acts.

There is a kind of philosophy about Islamophobia because every time there is a terrorist attack, such as September 11th and the Boston Marathon bombing, you will see a big news article about it. It makes some people feel uncomfortable around people wearing traditional Islamic clothing.

I studied a different school of philosophy that teaches the opposite way of thinking. In communist nations such as North Korea, there is no freedom of press, freedom of speech, or freedom of religion. All the news is government propaganda. What the people listen to and read is anti-West. Not only is our dress code different from theirs, but we are a different race and nationality. They are educated and taught to hate America from the time they are infants because the North Korean regime has been controlling this nation since WWII ended. Their parents and their grandparents could tell them anti-West ideas as well.

Some Muslim-majority countries have propaganda against the West just like North Korea, especially Iran. In 2017, the BBC did a study recently that says that Iranian people hates America more than any other country. This is an incomplete report. In this report, a lot of countries are missing, such as North Korea, Iraq, and Somalia. I believe the reason is because the BBC does not want to send reporters into an extremely anti-American country because the reporters may be jailed or shot.

China during the Mao era was almost like North Korea today. After Mao passed away in 1976, the politicians in China woke up and had political and economic reforms. Today's China looks so much more like South Korea, even the dress codes are almost identical. They are making a message without words that **China is allies with South Korea, but not North Korea**.

Eyewitness Cold War in China

I was born in Hong Kong. It was not controlled by Communist China until 1997. Hong Kong was a British colony and the people lived much better than the people living in Mainland China at the time. Even the dress code was different. We dressed much like westerners. In the past, there were movies which always had people in Eastern Asia wearing old-timey costumes. In reality, the people in some Eastern Asian countries such as Korea, Japan, and Hong Kong dress classier than the real westerners in Europe and America.

When I was a kid, the Americans were fighting the communists in Vietnam. China was giving the communists supplies including food, equipment, and weapons. The anti-American sentiment was extremely high in China. At the same time, there was a movement called the 'Cultural Revolution' in China. China was a very isolated country, but not as isolated as North Korea.

Hong Kong and Macau were western-controlled colonies. When China wanted to trade and communicate with the West, they used Hong Kong and Macau as a middleman. For the same reason, today's China let those two ex-colonies remain free, in case there was an embargo against China, they could still use those two special territories to communicate with the West.

My family had a routine. We went to visit our relatives in Mainland China once or twice a year. This is the story about my eyewitness account of Cold War China.

I was a little kid following my mom going to China to visit my relatives. The train must stop for the passengers to go through the customs checkpoint. The security was very tight, and under high alert. They searched all the luggage. Any reading materials must go through inspection so they may make sure there is no "corrupted" material from the West. You cannot bring it past the checkpoint.

Somebody asked "What does it mean, corrupted material from the West?" The customs agent said "The westerners are living in the corrupted society. China is banning all the corrupted materials, so they may not get in China. There is more than just porn that counts as corrupted. Any materials that expresses a Western living style such pop music or the Beatles is considered corrupted. Also, no religious materials, such as Bibles, can be carried past the checkpoint."

After I left the train, I found that there are anti-west propaganda posters were posted everywhere. Chairman Mao's image are in most of those posters. His image is the sun. Under his image, there is anti-West propaganda. The people in China were dressed in uniform-like communist clothing. Some of the people, although they were not in military active duty, wore military-style all-green clothing with a communist armband. Because we were dressed so much like westerners, as soon as we left the train, there were people staring at us.

My relative's house was not distant from the train station. I expected that we would get a taxi to pick us up. I did not see any taxi cabs in the train station but tricycles. We paid some money for a ride. During the trip, I eye witnessed there were a lot of holes being dug on the streets. I asked the driver "Are you guys digging holes for the subway train?" He said "No. Those are bunkers." I asked "Is the country going to have war? Why are we digging bunkers?" "He said "We believe the American imperialists will invade China very soon. We have to prepare for the war."

After I arrived at my relative's house, I found that everything inside their house was very old fashioned. There was no TV and no refrigerator, though there was a radio. When I turned on the radio, I heard strange propaganda, including a fictional story about a little kid. When he was very ill, doctors said "Your illness is critical and we do not expect to be able to save you." In the West, if people were in the same situation, they would pray to God to help them, to send miracles to help them recover. The child instead prayed to Chairman Mao to help him recover. Shortly after, the miracle arrived, and he recovered gradually. I was not surprised the people believed Mao was God, because back in the day, the people treated their ruler, such as the Emperor of Japan, as God. Their ruler was not just a king or emperor, but God, and some people imagined Mao as God.

Suddenly, a neighbor knocked on the door. She had a letter in her hand and asked all the adults in the house to sign their name on the paper. This letter was a petition. There was a doctor who charged people money and operated a private practice. He was a surgeon and he knew certain secrets about eye surgery. He was the only doctor in China who could perform this particular kind of eye surgery. People badmouthed the doctor to Chairman Mao and claimed that his private practice overcharged patients. Mao ordered his execution. The petition was made the neighbors, which called for Chairman Mao to spare the doctor's life. Some of the adults in the house signed the paper immediately, but one of the guys said "I think it is already too late. I believe before the letter reaches the post office, the doctor will already be executed. Kim Jong-Un has the same authority as Mao did. The difference is Mao would kill somebody just by ordering their execution. They died with one bullet, but Kim Jong-Un is a bloodthirsty tyrant who likes to see somebody he doesn't like blown up by artillery fire.

One of my cousins was about the same age I was. I was approximately 10 year old at the time. It was very common for a little boy to play with a toy gun. My cousin, while he was not a soldier, liked to wear an all green military uniform. When I asked about a toy gun, he went to his room and showed me a pistol. I asked "This is great! This gun looks real!" He said "This is a real gun." I asked him "This is a real gun? Where did you get this?" He said "Some of my older friends had to do military practice shooting live bullets with a real gun. After they finished the military practice, they just stole the gun."

During this point in time, a lot of non-military people such as the older teenagers had to serve military training. This was involuntary training. The government wanted to make sure if America invades China, everybody would know how to pick up a gun and fire.

It was summer break at the time. I asked my cousins if I could read their books. He gave me his schoolbook, including comic books. I was not surprised all the schoolbooks were covered in anti-West propaganda, but I was surprised how the comic books for little kids were too.

I remember one of the comic books was talking about Vietnamese child soldiers who were trained to kill Americans. The little kids learned to fire guns, including sniper rifles. They trained the children how to burry landmines and make traps, and how to get Americans to fall in the traps. As an example, there was an American commander who went into a village and asked a little kid "Did you see anybody carrying guns and hiding somewhere?" The little kid pointed his finger to somewhere and said "Somebody in there has a machine gun." When the commander looked to where the little kid was pointing, the little kid picked up a handgun and shot him to death.

One of my uncles was a communist transportation official. He said that he travelled all over China, and was in charge of some of the railroad systems. He told us stories about how there are trains loaded with weapons from Russia, transported through China, into Vietnam. The Chinese government was supporting the Vietnamese Communists. They allowed those trains to pass through China and into Vietnam without inspection. China was also giving the North Vietnamese Communists weapons, equipment, and food.

It was very often for the trains carrying farm products to stop for fuel, and find that there were people getting on the train and trying to steal farm products. He secretly ordered the train crew "Allow people to steal farm products. Don't call the police and do not report it to anybody. We do not have enough food to feed our own people. Those trains are headed for Vietnam. They will give the food to the Vietnamese for free. Our own people need to be fed. We would be better off giving the food to our own people rather than the Vietnamese."

I asked my uncle "how come people have to steal from the train if there is a food shortage in China?" He answered "No, we don't have shortage of food. The real problem is we are feeding our friends and neighbors, especially North Korea and Vietnam. We want to make sure they have access to food, also able to fight the Imperialist invaders. We also store millions of tons of food in the bunkers. In case the Imperialist invaders drop nuclear bombs, the survivor have food to eat for a while.

I went out with my family as a child. The immediately identify me as a person from Hong Kong because of my clothing. Before the Chinese begin the economic expansion since late 1970's, the general public lack materials including food and clothing. I saw most people, even my relatives wear clothing old and much worn. My mom offer my relatives her old clothing. Some of my relatives would not accept it, because it was too classy and western. If they wear those clothes on the street somebody will not like it, Mao's government perpetrates anti-western propaganda.

Here was an unwritten law in Mao's China. Just like in North Korea today, the people have to dress in plain colors, uniform like clothing. The reason is because they want to separate and distant themselves from the polluted western society. Even dressing like a westerner could be criticized as unpatriotic, although it is not a crime it was not socially acceptable. Just like somebody in the west dressing like a hippie.

We went to a restaurant with my relatives. My mom and I sit with my relatives. When the waitress came, my mother and I could order anything we desire. But the waitress asked my extended family food rations card. I asked for an explanation of what was going on. The residents of China cannot buy food or go to a restaurant without a food ration card. We are exempt from this because we are from Hong Kong. In China, at the time, all supplies and food must be measured and accounted for. This is true for the vast majority of supplies. For example to buy a bed, one must apply to the government, and the wait is long, six months, sometimes a year.

On the issue of television, I was told by my relatives they never see a TV ever. I suggest we bring one TV to China. However the TV is worthless without satellites signal. Long range fish bone antenna was banned in Mao's era. Watching all foreign TV was banned in China but it was never strictly enforced. As an example, there is radios in China, unless you are living very close to the Hong Kong border, you are able to receive broadcast signal in

Hong Kong. Of course movies are limited to majority of Chinese made movies. Here is the exceptions: some non-political America movies were allowed in theaters. Those movies are very old, such as Charlie Chaplain movies.

International, Hong Kong and Macau is the middle man for trade and communication. If one has caring relatives he can you with luxury items such as a TV, there was not able to receive broadcast from Hong Kong, there a local TV stations. The hotel showcases propaganda films on the TV. There is a death penalty if a North Korean watches South Korean TV.

Finally, the situation changed. People smuggle long range fish bone antennas to China. People living in Southern China, close to Hong Kong, are able to receive TV broadcast signals. Since the Hong Kong entertainment business is popular. Normally when somebody is watching the Hong Kong TV, as long as they can get a broadcast signal law enforcement will not be concerned, since the policemen are apathetic, and they like to watch the same channel. The human rights violation against freedom in today's North Korea is much worse than in Mao's China.

I asked if telephone service in China was present. There is telephone service but not to residential use. It is limited for government officials or some business such as a hotel.

The above story seems a lot like traveling with a time machine, to send North Korea to early 1970's China. **I believe the North Korean situation is worse than previous circumstances that happened in China.** At that time, I remembered we could purchase meat (pork, chicken and duck). Today North Korea households are rare to have access to meat.

In the 1970's there was not enough electricity to fuel a refrigerator. There was only enough electricity for the lighting. There was ice cream shops in the city, and access to dairy is in the stores. In North Korea there shortages of meat and dairy. If there is no refrigerator. Fresh meat and milk and ice cream could not be kept cold.

China has communist allies and friends, plus Hong Kong and Macau. Professional diplomates such as the Prime Minister Zhou Enlai and Deng Xiaoping try to improve the International relationship. As a result even in the toughest time China is not facing drastic sanctions. However North Korea is much isolated.

Starting in the early 1970s, the Chinese diplomats had been consistently working to break through their isolation. They replaced Taiwan as the permanent Security Council, invited Nixon to visit China and sign several agreements, and began having normal trade and diplomatic relationships with Japan. Shortly after, the Japanese started giving excessive help in reforming

China's economy. Capitalism is the path to bringing China from a poor, backwards agricultural nation to a wealthy, modern, industrial nation.

No one would expect North Korea to have the same change soon. Capitalism is a major taboo in North Korean politics. If any politician dares to mention capitalism, Kim Jong-Un will blow him up with heavy artillery. Nobody wants to help North Korea because no one wants to risk their lives in helping such a xenophobic country. A famous example: few years ago, an American visitor Otto Warmbier tried to steal a North Korean propaganda poster and was arrested, jailed, and tortured before he eventually died. The anti-America movement in North Korea must be very strong.

Prime Minister Zhou Enlai was the longest serving prime minister in China. He serves at the same time as Mao did (1949-1976). People in China believe Zhou Enlai was the best foreign diplomate in all of China's history. It accelerated China's break away from isolation. One of the biggest contribution for the communists, he negotiated for America's retreat from Vietnam, as well as the ceasefire in the Korean Peninsula (1953). North Korea lacks of such spectacular diplomates.

Fuel is important for military supplies and civilian transportation. China is large country with domestic oil wells. Due to economic expansion, today, China needs to import oil. Before the 1990's China is able to pump more oil than what was needed domestically. North Korea is a small country and a lot of supplies don't produce on their own. After the international sanction begins, they only receive drastically limited supplies of fuel.

Lack of food, fuel, material and entertainment is a harsh reality for today's North Korean citizens. This situation is not going to resolve at any time in the future, because the Cold War in China ended since the late 1970's. It never ended in North Korea.

During the Mao era, China did not have freedom of speech as restricted as today's North Korea. I read a lot of internet articles talking about Chinese tourists who went to visit North Korea. The North Korean government tries to separate the Chinese tourists from the local people, and does not allow them to communicate. During the Mao era, if a foreigner went to China, including a reporter, there was nobody to follow them and make sure they do not talk to anyone.

The High Tide of the Cold War

One day in the early 1970's I followed my mom and went to China and visited my relatives. Although I was a little kid at that time, I was more advanced than most children. I understand that nation is preparing to war.

One of my cousins was a strong young man. After he graduated high school, the communist government assigned him a job. Just like other people who live in communist nations, they don't have the freedom to look for their own job and are assigned jobs they do not like. The job assigned to him is to collect human waste. It sounds pretty awful, but he had no other choice.

One day, while we were eating dinner together, he stood up and announced "Today, I was accepted to the active military service. I am going to leave my awful job." One of my relatives said "Do you know there is a lot of tension today? I thought we were going to send troops to fight Americans in Vietnam, and you're going to active duty right now?" My cousin said "We don't have enough food to put on the table. If I go to the military, at least I could be well fed every day. After I leave the military, they will assign me to a better job."

My uncle asked "In the recruitment station, are there other people who want to join the military?" My cousin said "Yes. There are hundreds of young men and women in the recruitment station. They don't take every one of us. I am proud of myself for passing the exam, and it proves I am not weak. I know there will be an anti-imperialism protest tomorrow. If anyone wants to come see the protest, follow me tomorrow."

The next day, I followed my cousin to see the anti-imperialism protest. Before I left, I asked my mom to come with me, but she refused. She just got her hair permed not too long ago in Hong Kong and the clothing she wore was too western-style. If she went to see the protest, her dress code may work against her. I was a little kid, so it didn't matter.

There were thousands of spectators watching the protest on the street. In front of the protestors, there were a few columns of fully-armed soldiers. They carried AK-47 assault rifles and other kinds of handheld weapons. Behind them, there were a couple jeeps and military utility trucks. Those vehicles were armed with mounted guns and soldiers. Behind the vehicles were effigies of then-American president Richard Nixon and Uncle Sam.

They were holding guns and bombs. Behind them was a model of a B-52 bomber. Behind it were actors who represented casualties from the Vietnam War. They were wearing clothing with blood stains. Behind those actors were thousands of people following them. Each one was carrying signs protesting the Vietnam War.

The protestors and the spectators were screaming "Down with American imperialism!" They had signs and anti-American propaganda posters all over the streets. My cousin told me similar kinds of protests happened in every major city and this kind of protest was very frequent.

I asked him if any of my relatives had a camera. He said "We have cameras at home, but nobody dares to take a picture of the protest. Special permission is required, especially when there is military equipment on the street. If somebody takes a picture of the military equipment without permission, they could be accused of being a spy."

I asked my cousin "This is the high-tide of the Vietnam War. If you join the military, do you know where you will be deployed to?" My cousin said he didn't know. He had some classmates who joined the military before him. Some of them were sent to Hainan Island.

Hainan Island is the largest island is the South China Sea. It is almost as big as Taiwan. It is right next to North Vietnam. During the Vietnam War, the Hainan Island became a very important flash point and strategically important. If China decided to get involved in the war, the Hainan Island would have been a battlefield must fight.

Geographically, Hainan Island served as a natural barrier for the American fighters and bombers in launching airstrikes against North Vietnam. If the American war planes had to drop bombs to attack Hanoi, the B52 heavy bombers could take off in Okinawa or Guam. The naval aircrafts can take off from the aircraft carriers sailing in the Pacific Ocean. Hainan is just to the east of Hanoi and blocking the route. If the American war planes passed the air space above Hainan, the Chinese air defense system could shoot them down. During the Vietnam War, several American war planes were shot down in the Hainan air space. If the war planes had tried to avoid Hainan and headed south around the island, because the distance would be so much longer, they would have had to reduce their bomb loads.

Even if the American war planes flew en route to avoid Hainan, the long range air defense radar in Hainan could have tracked them down and sent an early warning to the North Vietnamese. The North Vietnamese' fighter jets and air defense missiles would be ready to counter the US airstrikes.

If the Chinese Government decided to join the Vietnam War, the entire South China Sea, including all the American military bases located in South

Vietnam and Philippian would be under the shadow of the air strikes by the Chinese air force bases located in Hainan.

Yulin's naval base is located in the south side of Hainan Island is the southernmost harbor in China. Despite China not having aircraft carriers at that time, it was one of the most important naval bases in China. The Chinese Naval vessels based in Hainan could launch naval blockade to all the seaports located in South Vietnam.

The size of Hainan is much larger than Okinawa and is much closer to the mainland. If American decided to launch an amphibious attack to take Hainan would be almost suicidal. The Chinese ground troops can transport from the mainland to Hainan much easier than the Japanese try to send additional troops to defend Okinawa during WWII since Okinawa is too far from Japan, from the mainland to Hainan is a short ride.

The massive build up for the Chinese combat troops in Hainan, including the most advanced air defense systems and warships. If the Chinese decided to become actively involved in the Vietnam War, Hainan Island would become the front line. It could face attacks from America and South Vietnam. My cousin said they already knew what would happen, but they will join anyway. If he doesn't join military service, there would be no hope for him to change his life and career. He was assigned an awful job he doesn't like, and most of the people could not afford to go to college.

While I discussed the war with my cousin and suddenly somebody targeted me because of the western-style clothing I was wearing. Somebody pointed their finger at me and said "Hey look! There is a boy dressing like a westerner! He must be from Hong Kong!" Unexpectedly, there were about a dozen people staring at me. My cousin said "He is only a little kid. His parents dressed him this way. It's not his fault!" He escorted me out of the site.

The above experience reminds me of North Korea today. One of the major differences is the Chinese soldiers are well fed every day, but North Korean soldiers are malnourished. According to my cousins, the Chinese soldiers get meat at every meal. Today's North Korean soldiers very rarely get a meal with meat. Recently, one of the high ranking North Korean military officials was executed by Kim Jong-Un because he was overgenerous when giving his soldiers and their families extra food and fuel rations.

During the Vietnam War era, despite the fact that most of the Chinese people experienced food shortage, the army is well fed plus it donates too enormous supply of food to help feed the communists of Vietnam. There is a saying, "An army can't march on an empty stomach." I don't believe that today's the malnutrition soldiers of North Korean military can have great efficiency against the south.

Just before the American forces retreated from Vietnam the general public in China were so strongly believed that the Chinese government would join in the forces against America, just like they joined the Korean War in the past. However "their bark was much worse than their bite". They did not join the war.

During the Vietnam War, when the American pilots were shot down in Hainan after they parachuted out, they were captured. They were held as POWs for years. Until 1973, they were released together with other captured American pilots and other crucial members such as John McCain. This was held in North Vietnam. At the time, the plane of one captured American pilot was shot down in 1965 in Hainan and the pilot was detained for eight years.

The 2001 Hainan Incident

In April 1, 2001, an American EP-3E signals intelligence aircraft was involved in a mid-air collision with a Chinese J-8II jet fighter over the South China Sea. It became an international headline.

On that day, shortly after the American aircraft took off from Okinawa, the Chinese military long range air defense radar locked on and was tracking the route of this aircraft. The Chinese air defense commander ordered a pair of J-8II jet fighters to intercept the American surveillance aircraft. They were ordered to not attempt to shoot it down, only follow the plane. When the planes got too close, a collision occurred. The Chinese jet fighter was destroyed and the pilot was killed. The American civilian aircraft was damaged and took an emergency landing in Hainan.

After the incident, there was a lot of debate in the media. When I watched the TV, I found that a lot of people were called "experts", who had their minds set back to the Cold War era. They do not have updated knowledge about modern political science. Someone referred to as a "Chinese expert" said "The Chinese Government are keeping the 24 American air crew members as hostages. Such incidents reminds of the 1968 North Korea spy ship incident involving the USS Pueblo being captured by North Korea."

In January 23, 1968, the USS Pueblo, an American spy ship, sailed to offshore North Korea to collect intelligence information. The North Korean Navy opened fire on the ship, killing 1 crew member and injuring several more. The spy ship surrendered and the crew members were detained for months until the American Government apologized and guaranteed it will not happen again. The crew was released after that, but the ship remains in custody till this day.

Such incidents could have created turmoil for China and America's relationship. I believe it will not become a repeated incidence like the USS Pueblo. There was a totally unrelated incident back to 1999. When an American warplane launched airstrikes against Yugoslavia, the Chinese embassy in Belgrade was accidently targeted and bombed. It caused the deaths of 3 Chinese journalists and injured multiple others. This incident ignited anti-American protests worldwide for a period of time. Shortly after, the Chinese and American governments resolved this incident peacefully.

Since the Cold War had ended, China and America no longer see each other as enemies, but major trading partners. By the turn of the century, China expanded their industrial power rapidly. At the same time, the American business owners were looking for a solution to reduce manufacturing costs. China and America took advantage of each other. The American manufacturers moved their production lines to China for their low cost of labor, or simply just imported products from China instead of making it in America. China had tens of millions of people hired to manufacture industrial products.

There was no reason for either of these great nations to ignite a second Cold War. American diplomats told the media "It was an accident, and we want to prevent this accident from becoming an incident."

After the incident, the Chinese government demanded the American government apologize for causing this incident, but President George W. Bush though that America had the right to fly surveillance planes in international airspace, and that he had nothing to apologize for. Finally, the American ambassador sent a letter approved by George Bush stating they were "very sorry" a Chinese pilot died and "very sorry" that the US plane landed in China without permission.

Because their languages are different, there are two different versions of the letter. In the American version, the American government states they are "very sorry" twice. It does not mean they admit to doing wrong. If America used the word "apologize" it would mean they did something not legitimate.

In the Chinese version, they wanted the American government to admit to wrongdoing, but when the letter said "very sorry" twice, they believed it meant the Americans were apologizing in response to the incident. As a result, shortly after the letter was issued, the 24 members of the American flight crew were release, and their aircraft was returned shortly afterwards.

During a different era, a similar incident occurred, but with a different solution. Imagine if an American surveillance plane made an emergency landing in North Korea, Iran, or Saddam Hussein era Iraq. What would happen? Those nations have no diplomatic or trade relationship with America. If a similar incident occurred, since their relationship was ruined right from the beginning, they will not try to improve their relationship.

One of my coworkers was a high ranking navy official. When I discussed the Hainan Incident and the USS Pueblo Incident with him, he could not give me any comment. I told him "The admiral who sent the USS Pueblo should be court martialed and the superiors of the US surveillance plane should also be punished. Both incidents were caused by poor coordination. The spy ship and the surveillance plane had almost no weapons to defend themselves. Why is it that they were deployed nearby North Korea and China? There was no naval warship or jet fighter to escort them."

The USS Pueblo was a WWII veteran, which was launched in 1944. The engines are very low capacity, which have 500 horsepower each. The full load of this ship weighed 895 tons. This is 1.1 horsepower per ton. The maximum speed of this ship is 12.7 knots. In reality, depending on the load and weather condition, this ship could sometimes sail at the speed of 9 knots. Could the US Military send a faster and better ship than the USS Pueblo? The maximum speed of the North Korean torpedo boats were over 40 knots, how could USS Pueblo such a slow and old ship escape from the chase.

This vessel had two 12.7 mm Browning machine guns. For naval warfare, it may not even be considered as a weapon, since a pair 12.7 mm Browning machine guns are too small to make significant damage to the enemy's vessels. When the North Korean torpedo boats and submarine chasers approached the USS Pueblo, the captain ordered to escape at maximum speed. The communist sailors recorded the USS Pueblo leaving at a speed of 9 knots. It is possible, because this ship was old and loaded.

The captain of the USS Pueblo immediately asked for the US Military to send aircrafts and warships to help. Despite America having the biggest navy on earth, no help arrived. The North Korean Military captured this ship easily. I believe the admiral in charge of the West Pacific operation at the time should have been court martialed.

For the Hainan Incident, it was the repeated mistake. The EP-3E signal intelligence aircraft is a slow-moving and large target. It is not a jet, but a 4 engine turboprop with a maximum speed of 780 km per hour, and no weapons for defense. There is no way this kind of aircraft could escape when facing the opposite side's jet fighters. During this operation, why did the Americans not send any fighter jets to escort this slow-moving target? If it was a secret operation, if the aircraft looked like a jetliner or another form of civilian plane, the opposite side may not be able to identify it as a spy plane. EP-3E is a military plane which looks obviously different from a civilian aircraft. If the opposite side could identify it is a military plane, it should have been escorted by jet fighters to avoid interception.

The Hainan Incident made the American military suspend the surveillance operation in South China Sea for a period of time, until finally they restored the operation. They sent faster surveillance planes, which were Boeing P8 jets, with McDonnell Douglas F-18 jet fighters to escort.

In 1969, a similar event happened. This time, an American EC-121 reconnaissance aircraft was shot down by North Korean MiG-21 jet fighters. The incident took place 167 km off the coast of North Korea. It caused the deaths of 31 crewmembers. After the incident, the American Government made little response. Why is it the Hainan Incident provoked such a larger American response, but not the 1969 spy plane incident? There are some reason:

North Korea does not have diplomatic or trade relationships with America. It is a hostile country towards America. Unless the American Government would take military action such as dropping bombs on North Korean military bases, there are not a lot of tools to retaliate, since the relationship was already bad. As an example, you cannot have sanctions or embargo to North Korea at that time because North Korea had little trade with the Western Allies. China, Russia, and Eastern Europe were major North Korea supporters, and they would give North Korea business and material supplies if an embargo took place.

Today's North Korea no longer has major support by those communist nations. It is the major reason the North Korean people were starving as soon as the Cold War ended. China is a very important trading partner for America. If a hostage crisis occurred, America could retaliate against China easily. For example, the American Government could put tariffs on Chinese imported products if China did not release the American crewmembers. Not until 2018 did the American Government put tariffs on Chinese imported products. It is for a totally unrelated reason. The American consumers and businesses need the low-cost Chinese products and the Chinese needed the American markets and money.

1969 was the high tide of the Vietnam War. Since America was fighting such an unwinnable war for years, Richard Nixon did not want to start a second front, like the Germans against the Russians and Western Allies at the same time, which caused the defeat of the German military. If America made military retaliation against North Korea, it could ignite a second Korean War. At the time, North Korea was backed by two major allies: China and the Soviet Union.

All 31 crew members of the EC-121 died after the plane was shot down. If the plane was damaged at made an emergency landing or landed in Cold War era China or Soviet Union, it would become a hostage crisis. The American Government would have to negotiate with those hostile countries and try to bail out those captured crew members. If all the crew members died on the scene, no hostages could be taken.

The Battle of the Paracel Islands

During the Korean and Vietnam War, the Chinese Navy never initiated a battle against the American Navy. In 1974 there was a battle between the Chinese Navy and the South Vietnamese Navy. It is the first naval battle the Chinese Navy launched against a foreign country since the communists controlled China in 1949.

In this battle the Chinese claimed an overwhelming victory. The reason was not because of the quantity or quality of Chinese weapon systems, but because the quality of Chinese soldiers were much superior to South Vietnam's. The maintenance of the weapons system, the training of the soldiers, and their will to fight were crucial steps leading to victory. The weapons themselves were without routine maintenance and were used by poorly-trained soldiers, who lacked the will to fight. It would not be possible to combat against the enemy effectively. The American weapon systems provided to South Vietnam were superior to the weapon systems provided to the North Vietnamese by the Chinese and Russians. Shortly after the American military retreated, the corrupted South military immediately collapsed and surrendered.

In the past, China held control of remote islands. Since the Ming Dynasty and possibly earlier, because these islands are far from the mainland and very small, they were seen as holding too little value to fight for them. In early 1974, before the battle began, some of those islands were controlled by the Chinese and some were controlled by the South Vietnamese government.

In 1973, the treasure and troubles of the islands arrived simultaneously. Oil was discovered on the islands. The South Vietnamese government declared that oil drilling will begin. As soon as the news arrived in Beijing, the Chinese government immediately sent a wakeup call to send the military and ordered them to reclaim this long forgotten territory.

In January 1974, a small Chinese fleet was sending weaponry to the army which was stationed in the islands. This was not a major combat fleet. These vessels were very small and had no intention of engaging in a major battle against any foreign country. No major service ships were present in the small fleet. This fleet included two Type 6605 Minesweepers, which had a displacement of 570 tons each. The fleet also included two Kronshtadt-class submarine chasers, which each had a displacement of 320 tons. Behind them were two types 037 Submarine chasers which each weighed 400 tons.

When the small Chinese fleet got close to the islands, the South Vietnamese Naval combat fleet engaged the Chinese fleet. Their warships were much bigger than the Chinese vessels they engaged. The South Vietnamese fleet included two destroyers. The flagship HQ-05 had a displacement of 2,592 tons. The other destroyer, an HQ-16, had a displacement of 2,551 tons. A corvette HQ-04 had a displacement of 1,590 tons. An Admiral-class Minesweeper HQ-10 had a displacement of 650 tons.

Everybody knows that South Vietnamese soldiers were famous for being timid and lacking motivation in battle. However in this case the ships of the South Vietnamese navy were obviously much bigger than the Chinese vessels. The South Vietnamese Naval Commander believed he could easily prevail over the smaller Chinese vessels. He ordered his ship to fire the first shot. Below are records of the strengths of both fleets.

1. Four Vietnamese naval vessels. Three of them were major surface combatants, plus one minesweeper. All six Chinese major vessels were very small. No major surface ship was present at the time. Two of them were minesweepers.

2. The total displacement for the South Vietnamese fleet weighed 7,383 tons (full load displacement). The total displacement for the Chinese weighed 2,580 tons, excluding two submarine chasers, which arrived late. Those four vessels only had a combined displacement of 1780 tons, less than one of the South Vietnamese destroyers.

3. There were four Chinese vessels engaged in battle in the beginning. There were two others which were too far away. They did not join this battle until it was at its last moments.

4. Two South Vietnamese naval destroyers: their main guns were the hard-hitting 127 mm naval guns. The largest gun for the Chinese vessels were the much smaller 85 mm naval guns.

5. The Chinese Navy has larger warships, such as guided missile destroyers. However none of them were present in this battle. Since this battle was not premeditated, the only weapon both fleets ascertained against each other were the naval guns.

If someone was never told the end result of this battle, an assumption would be surmised that the South Vietnamese won easily. In real battle, there was a surprise victory for the Chinese. All three South Vietnamese major surface ships were damaged. One South Vietnamese minesweeper sank. Over 100 South Vietnamese men were killed, injured or captured. The Chinese have two minesweepers which were damaged, but not sunk. Two submarine chaser suffered minimal damages. 18 Chinese navy men were killed.

Below were combat situations in this battle:

There are many different types of projectiles naval guns can fire. When the South Vietnamese navy fired the guns at the Chinese vessels, they lacked knowledge and training. They fired armor piercing projectiles against the Chinese vessels. Those heavy duty projectiles are designed to go against the enemy's armored ships, such as a cruiser. When it penetrates the small Chinese vessels, the projectile penetrates both walls of the vessel. Unless it hits the vessels under the water line it will inflict limited damage, only making two holes, one hole on each opposing chamber of the vessel.

The Chinese navy men are well trained and understand the different purposes and kinds of projectiles. When the guns are fired against the opposing naval ships with high explosive rounds, this kind of projectile (which is filled with dynamite) hits the target, the dynamite detonates and causes serious damage to the ships and the people.

Some of the South Vietnamese ships' guns never fired a shot because of a malfunction. In the Chinese fleet, almost all of the naval guns could fire immediately. Only one gun was jammed, and because the proper training of the Chinese navy men, it took them seconds to clear the jam and open fire.

The commanders of the Chinese Navy understood the weaknesses of a major surface ship. Because Chinese vessels are much smaller, it would not be easy to sink the South Vietnamese major surface ships. If you destroy the enemy's firing control system, the enemy naval guns would become blind. The first target for the Chinese naval vessels were the South Vietnamese radar antennae. Those antennae were not protected by armor and were large targets. As soon as the Chinese knocked down those antennae, the Vietnamese vessels were not able to fire accurately.

There was a miracle during the sea battle. When the sea battle begun, there were four vessels on each side, with each warship fighting one-on-one. One of the Chinese minesweepers, hull #389, had a displacement of 570 tons and fought against a South Vietnamese warship, HQ-16. HQ-16 was an American-made destroyer which had a displacement of 2,551 tons. Minesweepers are not considered major combat vessels, only auxiliary naval ships. Not only were the guns much weaker, but the maximum speed of this Chinese ship was only 14 knots.

When the battle begun, both vessels fired cannons at each other. Because the training of the Chinese was much better, they were almost able to beat the enemy destroyer, which was much bigger than the minesweeper. In the middle of the battle, the 85mm main guns of the minesweeper ran out of ammunition. The captain of the minesweeper ordered for the vessel to ram the

South Vietnamese destroyer. When they closed in, because the minesweeper carried infantry weapons intended for delivery to the Chinese soldiers on the islands, the sailors used those weapons, including machine guns and rocket propelled grenades, to attack the South Vietnamese vessel. When the Chinese ship got even closer, it almost rammed in to the destroyer, the Chinese sailors were able to throw hand grenades onto the South Vietnamese destroyer. The destroyer increased its speed and fled the battlefield. After the warship arrived in South Vietnam, they inspected it and found 820 holes.

After the battle ended, the captain of the minesweeper received military rewards because **throughout naval history, this was the only time a minesweeper was able to defeat a destroyer**. Such a miracle from the naval combat history became an icon. It appeared in the Chinese art works including large fine paintings. This story made to become a movie.

I believe there must have been some maintenance problems with the destroyer HQ-16. Unless this ship's engines were badly damaged during the battle, it should have been able to escape before the minesweeper could close in and throw grenades on the deck. Because the maximum speed of the minesweeper was only 14 knots, the poor maintenance could have been the reason the South Vietnamese lost this battle.

When the South Vietnamese commander discovered there are two Chinese submarine chasers heading to the battlefield. He ordered his fleet to retreat. The smallest and weakest South Vietnamese vessels, HQ-10, a minesweeper, was not able to move fast and was left behind. Two brand new Chinese 037 class submarine chasers were moving at maximum speed, 30 knots, towards the slow-moving minesweepers. The submarine chasers caught up and opened fire, sinking the minesweepers easily.

After the naval battle ended, the Chinese launched an amphibious attack to take the two of the Paracel Islands, which were controlled by the South Vietnamese. There were no gun battles on the Paracel Islands during the Chinese amphibious operations. In one of the island, before the Chinese soldiers landed, the Chinese naval vessels fired their cannons at the South Vietnamese occupied island. As soon as the Chinese soldiers landed, the South Vietnamese soldiers raised the white flag and surrendered. They found that one of the POWs was an American.

On the other island, when the Chinese soldiers landed, the Vietnamese soldiers had evacuated without a trace. Several days later, they found those Vietnamese soldiers had landed in South Vietnam, but some of them had starved to death due to being lost at sea.

The South Vietnamese soldiers said when they saw the Chinese warplanes arrive, they believed the Chinese would launch an amphibious attack soon. They did not wait for South Vietnam to send vessels to rescue them. Instead, they fled the island on lifeboats. In reality, the Chinese warplanes flew above the islands as part of a reconnaissance mission. They took pictures of the island, but did not drop bombs. Because those soldiers had no will to fight, they did not fire a single shot before fleeing the islands.

Some may ask "What happened to the Chinese major naval surface combatants?" During the Vietnam War, most of the large Chinese warships were located in the North. There are major cities such as Beijing and Shanghai which are located near the Korean Peninsula which had to be protected. For the Chinese military, they believed they were facing the Americans on three fronts: Korea, Taiwan, and Vietnam. Because Vietnam is far away from the Chinese heartland, Beijing and Shanghai, they put almost all of the major surface ships in the North. Shortly after the Battle of the Paracel Islands, the Chinese Navy sent a fleet of major surface ships across the Taiwan Strait to the South China Sea.

During the battle, the South Vietnamese officials asked the American Navy Seven Fleet to deploy air craft and naval warships to join the fight against the Chinese military. Despite the Seventh Fleet having a large amount of warships sailing in the West Pacific at that time. They refused to join the fight.

Before Nixon visited China in 1972, the American Government was looking for solutions and opportunities to pull out from the Vietnam War. Since the "Paris Peace Accords" signed on January 27th, 1973, the American Government doesn't want to come back to Vietnam to fight again, takes no action.

The American POW who was captured on the island was an embarrassment to the American politicians. Before the incident, the Chinese government had a secret agreement with the American politicians stating both North Vietnam and China will release the American POWs. In exchange, the American military would have to retreat from Vietnam. The single captured American POW was released shortly after the battle ended.

To win or lose a war or battle, not including the weapons, the soldiers, or the commanders, the most important part is the highest command. A famous example is Hitler vs. Stalin. During WWII, the Nazi German soldiers were famous for being tough fighters because Hitler would know how to push his generals to fight hard. But Stalin was even tougher. If the high command officials refused to fight, he may be either jailed or killed by Stalin. During the Russian-German War, the Red Army had much higher casualties than the Nazis, but finally Russia declared victory despite suffering the highest casualty of all the nations which joined WWII.

When the South Vietnamese fleet commander Colonel Ha Van Ngac retreated back to South Vietnam, he was interviewed by President Nguyen

Van Thieu. To not embarrass himself and his navy, he made up lies. He told the media and the president they were engaged in furious fights with Chinese major surface ships, including a guided missile destroyer. When the Chinese guided missile destroyer fired missiles to sink the minesweeper HQ-10, he knew that they would not be able to win the fight. To avoid another warship being sunk by the Chinese missiles, he ordered they retreat back to South Vietnam.

President Nguyen Van Thieu didn't punish him, and showed sympathy and promised he would give him a replacement for the loss. If President Nguyen Van Thieu had the same personality as Hitler, he would be jailed. If he had the personality as Stalin, he would get shot. This is not the end of the embarrassment. A year later, when South Vietnam was going to lose the war and be conquered by the communists, the South Vietnam Navy did not join the fight. The warships HQ-5 and HQ-16 fled to the Philippines.

Although the battle was relatively small, we can learn that during the Vietnam War, China was well prepared for war. The soldiers of the Chinese military had more morale when engaging in a fight.

Air War Against America

During the sixties and seventies, there were almost ten thousand American aircrafts lost in Vietnam, Laos, Cambodia, and China, but mostly in Vietnam. Many people may be confused as to how it is possible for a country as small and poor as Vietnam was able to shoot down so many American aircrafts. Decades after the war ended, some secret documents were declassified. A lot of American aircrafts were not shot down by the Vietnamese, but by the Chinese.

At the time, Americans were afraid the Vietnam War will expand. They tried to prevent the Chinese military from joining in like in the Korean War. The Chinese were also afraid the war would expand to China. When the Chinese government sent people to Vietnam, they served as air defense crew and the military labor to set up air defense systems. They were not allowed to serve in ground combat on the front lines, as they could be captured. There were 320,000 Chinese military personnel or non-combatant laborers serving in Vietnam. 4,000 of them died during the mission.

I do not believe when China sent out such a large number of people, America did not know about it. The American government may have wanted to leave room for negotiating with the communists. Right from the beginning of the war, the American government had no intention to win. This was the biggest mistake of the Vietnam War. This is the reason America and South Vietnam lost the war.

One of the reasons America lost so many aircrafts in Southeast Asia is because America believed their air force technology was vastly superior to the communists. An example is when five U-2 aircrafts were shot down in China, four of those planes became exhibits in the Military Museum of the Chinese People's Revolution. I used to watch TV and read many books and magazines published in America. They state U-2 high-tech reconnaissance aircrafts were the most advanced aircrafts during the 1950s. There is no way the communists could possibly shoot them down. The aircrafts must have malfunctioned and crashed. Not until decades after the Vietnam War ended, the Chinese government declassified documents revealing those U-2's were shot down easily.

When the Chinese magazines discussed how they shot down the first

U-2, they disagreed with American sources, which claim the planes were undetectable. The Chinese air defense radar can spot and lock on a U-2 aircraft from very far away, and their anti-aircraft missiles were ready to fire.

On September 9th, 1962, The Chinese shoot down the first U2. The problem is the air defense commander requested his superior to approve shooting down the aircraft. His superior refused, but asked his superior the same request. Not until half an hour later, the Prime Minister of China, Zhou Enlai, received a phone call and approved firing missiles. The first shots hit, and the U-2 pilots was killed. Later on, 4 more U-2s were shot down in similar incidents.

Not including the U-2s, some other American warplanes such as A-6s, F-4s, F-104s, plus some unmanned aircrafts were shot down over China during the Vietnam War. One of the unmanned aircraft lost in China during the reconnaissance mission was Lockheed D-21 supersonic drone. Unlike U2 this is a true stealth aircraft. This can fly at a speed as Mach 3.35 as an operational altitude of 27,000 meters. It was the ultra-high tech most advanced reconnaissance vehicle at that time. After it lost it became an exhibit in the Chinese Aviation Museum. Not until 1972 when Richard Nixon visited China, he promised the Chinese officials America will to cease all the reconnaissance missions near and over China.

I studied philosophy. The rumors that the American U2 aircrafts are undetectable and impossible to shoot down are a modern fairytale. They were made up by some Americans trying to fool themselves. This kind of idea is called denial, which is very common. They refuse to believe some of the American military systems was outdated. They always believed the American military capacity must be superior. In fact the entire American weaponry is superior to any country in most systems. But not in every system. Some particular systems such as electronic warfare systems is lagging behind China.

The history could be repeated. I'm wondering, if such expensive aircrafts like the B-2, F-22 and the F-35 were also advertised as undetectable, and impossible to be shot down by the enemies missile, would they also be 21st Century fairytales?

In modern warfare, science and technology is one of the most important parts, especially air defense systems. Each generation of the air defense system is superior and capable of detecting and shooting the enemy aircrafts. On the opposite side, each generation of aircraft would be more difficult to detect and more difficult to shoot down by the enemy's air defense system.

As an example, during the First Gulf War in 1991, the Iraqi force are able to shoot down several American and other allies war planes, including F-18. F-18 Hornet is the most advanced aircraft deployed to the Persian Gulf region at that time.

Twelve years later, America and the British invade Iraq. There were no allies' air craft being shot down. Despite some aircraft such as A-10 or F-18 being shot down 12 years earlier during the First Gulf War. Because the American upgraded the electronic warfare system in those aircrafts. When the Iraqi fired the missiles toward the aircrafts, they missed the target.

When the History Channel says the U-2 is impossible to detect or shoot down with missiles, what kind of missile or radar system are they talking about? Today, a lot of people believe F-22, F-35, and B-2 stealth aircrafts are not able to be detected or shot down with missiles. Are they talking about the Cold War era Russian air defense system, or are they talking about the most modern Russian and Chinese air defense systems?

When I review the Chinese media, some authors swear the modern Chinese air defense system has anti-stealth radars and can detect and identify a stealth aircraft several hundreds of kilometers away. They have long range anti-aircraft missiles, and can shoot down the American stealth aircrafts, such as the B-2, F-22 and F-35. When one side talk about how advanced their aircraft is and believe there is no way it can be detected or shot down. On the opposite side they talk about how advanced or their radar or missiles are and can detect and shoot down any aircrafts. Who is wrong and who is right. The only way to find out is to attempt it.

Since the Cold War was over, there have been little chance for the major superpowers take military action against each other. North Korea is no longer Chinas military allies, but are political allies. Unless there are substantial change, there is no chance China is selling the most advanced anti-stealth anti-aircraft system to North Korea.

Iran is one of the biggest resource for the Chinese importation of oil. The American Government has no expert to study the China-Iran relationship. In the last few decades China has invested tens of billions of dollars to drill Iranian oil. There is no chance China will stop importing oil from Iran since there was too much invested.

China is the second biggest weapons supplier to Iran, behind Russia. To avoid retaliation from America, the weapons supplied to Iran are second class defensive system. The missiles are downgraded, the sensors, warheads, and range are all inferior to the missiles the Chinese use themselves. There have been rumors for years that China will supply J-10 or FC-1 jet fighters to Iran. This never actually happened. We can eliminate the possibility China will supply Iran with the most advanced anti-stealth radars and missiles. In a separate case, the Russians refused to sell the Iranian Su-30 fighter/bomber.

There are many countries, such as Cuba and Venezuela, which are as hostile towards America as Iran and North Korea. I hope the American Government will use diplomatic solutions to make sure China and Russia will not supply those advanced anti-stealth radars and missiles to anti-American countries.

During the Middle Eastern conflicts, the majority of Israeli aircrafts were made in America. A few of them were manufactured by American allies, such as France. Most of the Arab nations' military aircrafts used to fight Israel, were manufactured by the former Soviet Union or today's Russia. The most common form of jet fighters are the MiG series. Throughout several wars in the past, the Arab nations suffered heavy losses in their air forces. The losses of the Israeli Air Force were significantly less than those of the Arabs.

Somebody came to the conclusion that the American jet fighters are by far superior to the Russian MiGs' jet fighters. This is not accurate. The performance of the MiGs in the East Asian battlefield operated by the Chinese and North Vietnamese pilots had a much better performance against the American aircrafts.

Modern air warfare is very complicated. It involves more than just pilots and aircrafts. Ground control, radar surveillance, antiaircraft missiles and guns, electronic warfare equipment, the training of the maintenance crew, the response of the commanders, and political issues are all key factors in determining the performance of the air force.

The poor performance of the Arab states air force, may be because the Middle Eastern soldiers were not trained as well as the Chinese and North Vietnamese soldiers. Some of the military failures could be caused by lack of intelligence or the top command such as the president of the nations, won't heed the warnings. Before the Pearl Harbor attacks, the Chinese intelligence predicted an attack. This warning was ignored by President Franklin Roosevelt and his high officials. Before the Pacific war began, they were overly confident, the Japanese won't dare to start a war against America.

During the 1967 Six-Day War, the Israeli air force launched a sudden attack against the Arab states air force. Within hours, most of the Arab's military aircraft were destroyed on the ground with no chance to take flight. It could be caused by the intelligence failure for the Arab states. They were not prepared for this sudden attack.

The Six-Day War was a miracle for modern air warfare. At that time the Israeli air force have not received advanced American warplanes yet. The aircrafts they used were made by the French which were a little less advanced than the American aircraft from the same generation. Israel only lost 46 aircrafts in this war, the Arabs lost 452 aircrafts. The losses were ratio at 1 to 10.

One of the reason for the Israeli air force successes was because not just the pilot was well trained, but also were the maintenance crews on the ground. A modern military jet is different than an automobile. A commercial automobile such as a taxi cab or bus you just need to have the drivers control the automobiles and add fuel to the vehicle. There is no need to change the motor oil for months only need to go to repair shop if there is a problem.

A modern military jet is a very complicated and expensive machine. Some aircraft parts need to be routinely inspected and replaced after the battle. If a car or truck has a mechanical problem while in operation, it will break down on the road and a tow truck will need to be called for it to be taken to a repair shop. Unlike a grounded automobile, if a warplane breaks down during a flight, it will crash with a very high chance of killing the flight crew. Depending on the conditions of the war planes, the more the aircraft fling the more maintenance required. It is not unusual for every hour of flight, takes twenty hours for ground maintenance. During war time in the Arab states, if one war plane can take one mission a day would consider flying a substantial amount.

This rule does not apply to the Israeli air force. In the war time the Israeli war planes take combat missions several times each day. As soon as an Israeli war plane landed after a combat mission, the ground crew immediately refilled the plane and reloaded the weapons. The war plane took off again and continue other combat mission. Even the American air force the ground maintenance is no match for the efficiency of the Israeli air force.

During the Shah era of Iran, Iran used to import hundreds of American war planes. After decades of sanctions and embargo against Iran, the Iranian air force American made F-14 Tomcat F-4 Phantom II and F-5 jet fighters lack of replacement parts. All of the vintage American war planes are over 40 years old are still the backbone of the Iranian air force today. Iran received a small number of Cold War era Chinese and Russian made jet fighters, they are outclassed compared a modern air force.

Lack of replacement parts is the major downfall of the Iranian air force. The pilots have to pass routine flight practice to become top gun pilots. Each aircraft has a maximum flight life. Most Cold War era Russian and Chinese-made fighter jets in Iranian air force are mostly disabled or have lived past their life expectancy. All the American-made Iranian war planes have passed their maximum flight life expectancy. In recent years, the Iranian air force has lost several aircrafts in incidents not related to combat, including the 2009 Iranian Air Force Il-76MD Adnan 2 accident. They lost their only airborne early warning and control aircraft.

Today, the inventory of the combat jets of the Iranian air force is down to no more than 200, including a small number of self-made Saeqeh-80/Kowsar jet fighters. Saeqeh-80/Kowsar jets are outdated designed jet fighters look alike the 1970s American Northrop F-5E Tiger jet fighter. Because of the poor efficiency of the Iranian aviation industry, only able to produce approximately a dozen Saeqeh-80s. If there is to be a war against Iran today, most of the Iranian aircrafts may not be able to take off and serve combat duty. Even if a few Iranian aircrafts can take off, due to the lack of training among fighter pilots and age of the aircrafts, their efficiency would be terribly poor.

After Iran fell to the Islamic militant regime in 1979, Saddam Hussein took advantage of the American arms and trade embargo against Iran and was at war with them from 1980 to 1988. Saddam Hussein proved the Iranian air force was neither better nor worse than the Iraqi air force. Both air forces were just as bad. The Iraqi air force was destroyed by America and its allies in the two Gulf Wars. In today's American air force, after decades of development, planes such as the F-4 and F-14 Jet Fighter, the F-111 Fighter/Bomber, the A-6 and A-7 and Naval Attacker, F-117 Stealth Bomber, have all been retired and replaced with more modern aircrafts. The air launched weapon and the electronic warfare system are updated to the latest techniques.

When reading books and internet articles, I am surprised that so many people with no military knowledge over exaggerate the Iranian and North Korean air power. If the American and the allies can be able to destroy Iraqi air force a few decades ago, it should be able to destroy both of the air force without difficulty.

Make Money Make Friends

Money can make friends, the modern China has the biggest goal to become an economic superpower. This is not necessary to become a military superpower like the former Soviet Union, exports communism and challenge the American military. They don't have a goal to invade other nations, because it would jeopardize the economic development they seek.

China's top five biggest trading partners plus North Korea trading data:

Country	Total trade	Export	Imports	Trade balance
United State *	635.4	505.5	129.9	+375.6
Hong Kong **	343.2	330.5	12.7	+317.7
Japan **	278.5	135.6	142.9	-7.3
South Korea **	275.8	101.3	174.5	-73.2
Taiwan ***	195.3	43.2	152.1	-108.9
North Korea **	5.5	2.9	2.6	+0.3

Source:

*US Census Bureau 2017: U.S. trade in goods with China.

**World Integrated Trade Solution 2015. China is the biggest trading partner for North Korea. Due to China joining international sanctions, the trading between China and North Korea has been decreased.

***Chinese Customs Report 2017. The money figure in this report is by Chinese yuan, One U.S. dollar is equal to 6.9 Chinese yuan.

The above data could explain to you, China is dependent on foreign trade. To improve quality of life of the people, improve their industrial power and economic power. American is Chinas biggest trading partner. Japan, South Korea and Taiwan are the major trading partner for China in the Far East, excluding Hong Kong. If China is ever involved in another military conflict, it will most likely be against Taiwan, South Korea, or Japan. The tens of millions of people working in the factories of China to produce export products will lose their jobs. The exports will be hit hard, as well as they will not be able to import quality, high tech products from those countries.

South Korea and Japan are American allies. Taiwan is an unofficial ally for America. If there is a major conflict between China and those countries, America will retaliate by reducing or shutting down trade with China or by increasing the tariffs for imported Chinese products. It would create economic turmoil in China.

A global trade war is not like WWI or WWII. We won't see blood on the battlegrounds, but it would make the tens of millions of casualties from the people employed by the manufacturers losing their jobs. If the problem is not able to correct the economic problem will grow to be a global problem. It can even ignite the second great depression. Of course, China won't sacrifice their economic well-being to help North Korea to invade the South.

Just before the sanctions against North Korea, the trade between China and North Korea was pretty small. If the Chinese did not trade with North Korea, the Chinese economy would not be hurt, and would not feel any pain.

China imports large amounts of goods from Japan, South Korea, and Taiwan without exporting as much to them, whereas the trade relationship between China and America is the inverse. Japan, South Korea and Taiwan has a positive trade relationship with China. When China imports high tech products from America the American politicians frequently set a road block to stop the trade. Japan, South Korea and Taiwan their politicians are rarely involved with trade deals. As a result the Chinese government and individual business owner would like to import high tech products, from those countries but not America.

A few decades ago all of the business men living in the "free world" believe China was an anti-capitalism communist extremist nation. Most wealthy people from the non-communist industrialized nations and they reluctant to invest in China. Japan led the way to breaking down barriers and began investing in China. After the Japanese tore down these barriers to investment, other industrialized nations followed. Today China receives more foreign investment than any other country.

China is the second biggest trading partner for Japan. The Japanese not just buying or selling huge amount of products to each other, Japan makes heavy investments to the Chinese industry. The aging population and the high cost of labor led to trouble with Japanese industry. Moving the manufacturing facility to China is one of the effective solutions.

The dispute of ownership of the Senkaku Islands have been on hold for several decades. So not to ignite diplomatic problem since they have a beautiful trade and business relationship, the islands are kept purposely vacant. There is no developments for future plans for both sides.

China is the biggest trading partner for South Korea. They established normal trade and diplomatic relationship since 1992. The amount of trade between China and North Korea is less than 2 percent than the amount of trade between China and South Korea. Before they signed a diplomatic and trade agreement, the Chinese Government promised to reduce the weapons sale to North Korea and they fulfilled the promise. The same situation like in Japan they put heavy investment in China.

Since the Chinese downgraded the relationship with North Korea, as a result it costs major economic turmoil for North Korea. And it costs millions of North Koreans to starve to death.

Since the communists control China in 1949 there have been categorized Taiwan as a land controlled by rebels. Today China is Taiwan's biggest trading partner. It counts for 30 percent of the total trade. Their political differences were put on the side and only discuss financial and business issues. The Chinese government no longer sends out threats to Taiwan like it did in the past, there is no chance recently, that China will invade Taiwan.

North Korean Nuclear Weapons

In recent years, despite international sanctions North Korea fired long range missiles and conducted several nuclear tests. If North Korea is targeting South Korea, they don't need to develop long range missiles. It is obvious they are targeting America. Unless Kim Jong-Un wants to kill himself together with millions of his own people, I don't believe he is rash and foolish enough to use his nuclear weapons. American will retaliate immediately.

Most people don't understand the technology of long range missiles. Their missile system are comparable to those of the 1960's, Russian nuclear missile system. This outdated system is obsolete, it is retired from the Russian inventory for decades.

Nuclear bombs and their launch vehicles are two different kind of weapons. Today, despite there are nine countries which own nuclear weapons they are America, Russia, China, England, France, India, Pakistan, Israel and North Korea have nuclear weapons, Only the first five countries have inter-continent nuclear strike capability. The other four (including North Korea) doesn't have full nuclear capability.

North Korea does not have the most advanced nuclear bombs, and their technology is very primitive. The first nuclear bomb was dropped in Hiroshima. Named Little Boy, it weighed 4400 kg. A B-29 heavy bomber had to be modified to carry this bomb. The modern nuclear bombs are much smaller. A long ranged missile is able to have multiple warheads stored inside the missile. The North Korean missiles have limited payloads. Since they don't have the advanced technology to make their hydrogen bombs smaller, their long ranged missiles can barely carry a single atom bomb.

If you fire an old-time missile into outer space, it is not easy to have the warhead land accurately to hit its target. The launch vehicle could be destroyed when it returns to the atmosphere, or the warhead will land too far away from its target. If North Korea dares to fire an ICBM at America, the American missile defense system will be able to track down and destroy the launch vehicle before it reenters the atmosphere, or a single atom bomb warhead will land far away from its target. Unless this is a hydrogen bomb with a very large killing radius, if a single atom bomb lands in a rural area or the ocean, there would not be significant damage. I believe North Korea is not able to make their hydrogen bombs small enough to be carried by a long range missile.

The other technique to attack your long distance enemies with nuclear weapons is a submarine launched missile. North Korea has one or two Sinpo-class diesel electric submarines, each capable of carrying two short range missiles. In modern warfare, Russia no longer use diesel electric submarines to carry nuclear missiles. Those outdated submarines are not able to stay submerged for a long distance. They must go to the surface to acquire air supplies. The North Korean submarines are too small to carry large missiles. If they want to fire those missiles at America, they would have to sail within the combat radius of the American coast. If they only carried two small short ranged missiles, it would not be worth the trouble to launch such a suicide attack. American anti-submarine warfare would be able to track down and sink North Korean submarines easily.

The other kind of nuclear attack technique is use of strategic long ranged bombers. In the olden days, nuclear bombs were carried by a warplane, and dropped directly onto the target, such as when America dropped atomic bombs on Japan. Today, because of the advanced air defense system, bombers no longer drop atom bombs like in WWII. Strategic long ranged bombers can carry cruise missiles. The warplanes fire cruise missiles far away from the target to avoid being shot down by enemy anti-aircraft fire. Typically, an air launched nuclear missile has a range between 1500-4000 km. North Korea has neither long range strategic bombers nor cruise missiles.

A modern warship could also fire nuclear capable cruise missiles to strike a long range target. North Korea does not have this kind of missile. Their warships are very small and lacking in anti-missile and air defense systems. If they dare to sail close to the American continent, the American military can sink their ship easily.

Nuclear weapons could become more of a hassle than a killing machine. After the Soviet Union collapsed, Ukraine became independent and gave up all of their nuclear weapons, long ranged missiles, and strategic bombers. If they did not decide to use them, why not just give it up?

In the past, Saddam Hussein decided to try to develop nuclear weapons. Israeli warplanes launched airstrikes to destroy the Iraqi nuclear facilities before the First Gulf War. After they lost the First Gulf War, to avoid international community from tightening their sanctions, they scrapped all of their weapons of mass destruction. After Saddam Hussein was overthrown and the allies liberated Iraq, there was no trace of weapons of mass destruction.

During the Trump, Kim Jong-Un meeting in Singapore, Kim Jong-Un promised he will give up his nuclear weapons. So far, there is no evidence this will come to fruition.

Weapons of mass destruction are very dangerous materials. When there is a nuclear test, radiation is left on the ground and can cause serious health issues, which can result in death. Chemical and biological weapons are different from dynamite. If there is a leak in the container, it could cause serious pollution. During WWI and WWII, there were accidental leaks of chemical weapons. It caused the deaths of civilians and military personnel.

During WWII, the Japanese 731 Unit located in Manchuria tested biological weapons. They would never dare to use this weapon on the Allies. The Japanese Government believed if they dared to use this weapon, the Allies could use the same techniques against Japan, and the germs they release could make their own people become victims.

In a democratic country, if there is a majority vote, we could have a vote to get rid of the politician in the next election. Kim Jong-Un is a cold blooded and brutal dictator. His own people are not able to overthrow him easily and get him out of office. Thousands of North Korean people have gotten ill or die because of nuclear tests. He does not care since nobody can tell him what to do, but I do not believe he would dare to use those weapons against the US as a suicide mission.

A Paper Tiger: North Korean Air Force

In the modern warfare the air superiority can make or break the end results of the entire war. In the past, smart weapon did not exist. The air dropped bombs free fall from the war planes. Most of them will not hit its target but cause massive civilian deaths. Even today the North Korean regime is still using massive amount innocent people die by airstrike during the Korean War as anti-American propaganda.

The two Gulf Wars prove that air launch smart weapons could strike the target with high success rate. Which side has the air superiority, which side can win the war.

The North Korean Airforce is a collection of outdated vintage jet museums. In 2014, when Kim Jong-Un visited his air force, they showed off some modern air crafts such as Su-25, MiG-27 and MiG-29. Vietnam War era MiG-17, MiG-19, and MiG-21 jet fighters are also in the base.

Same year, he took another visit to other North Korean air force base. There was a big surprise. In this visit the air crafts launched target practice were not jet fighters, but small noncombat aircrafts. A McDonnell Douglas MD 500 light utility helicopter was first to take flight. A Russian Antonov An-2 utility bi-plane shooting rockets to the target. After, a Nanchang CJ-6 propeller basic trainer showed up. None of them should serve combat duty.

It looks more like a joke than a military exercise. An-2 is a kind of low-cost, low maintenance, general purpose utility aircrafts. Like a flying mini-bus. The Chinese and Russian military use this kind of aircrafts as short range air travel, it also delivers mail and does paratrooper training. The maximum speed of those aircrafts is only 258 km/h. It is slower than a WWII Nazi Ju-87 Stuak Dive Bomber or a modern attack helicopter.

The Nanchang CJ-6 propeller basic trainer is one of the cheapest military trainers in the current international air-arm market. This aircraft is not very good to fly. The low purchase price, low maintenance cost and low fuel consumption made it become a popular aircrafts in the international arm trade. Most of the operators are the Third-World poor countries. It can only carry some light-weight weapons. You get the low quality product for the low price you pay for.

On September 9th, 2018, North Korea celebrated its 70th anniversary.

During the military parade, the aircrafts appeared in the sky. They were a bunch of ancient-looking bi-planes. Those aircrafts are the Russian Antonov An-2 utility aircrafts. Those planes haven't been manufactured for decades. It could mean the North Korean military lacked fuel, pilots lacked sufficient training and the maintenance crews lacked parts.

The modern military jet engines are high thrust, high tech, high fuel consumption, high maintenance, and high cost machines. A military jet engine has a life expectancy, the more it is used the faster it wears out. Both life expectancy and fuel efficiency for both Chinese and Russian made jet engines are inferior to the American made jet engines. The operation costs of a F-16 jet fighter is approximately $25,000 an hour.

An-2 and CJ-6 use piston engines. A piston engine is low cost in maintenance and low fuel consumption. The WWII war planes use piston engines. I surmise that the North Korean regime cannot afford the extensive high cost to fly the expensive military jets, they can only afford for limited operations.

In the previous section I used to talk about the poor performance of the Iranian air force. I give them a rating of D-. I would give North Korean air force a rating of D. America is the only air force on earth rated with an A. China and Russia are B. Japan, South Korea and Taiwan are C.

China and Russia are the two biggest weapons supplier to North Korea. America is the biggest weapons supplier to Japan, South Korea and Taiwan. The American air crafts are very different than the North Korean air craft. To understand how poor the North Korean air force is, we can compare the inventory of North Korea air crafts to the Chinese and Russians.

The North Korean air force have approximately 800 fixed wing combat jets. The biggest amount of air crafts are the Chinese Chengdu J-7 jet fighter. These are the Chinese version of Russian MiG-21 jets. There 120 J-7s and 26 MiG-21s. Both China and Russia shut down the production line of those aircrafts for years. Before the first Gulf War, the Iraqi air force also have many of those aircrafts. All the MiG-21s in Russia is already retired. Most J-7s in China are on the way out. If the allies can defeat the Iraqi air force back to 1991, they could defeat the North Korean air force now.

The Vietnam War eras MiG-17, MiG-19 Jet fighters and Ilyushin ll-28 light bomber are still in service. China and Russia no longer use these planes since many decades. Those aircrafts have no true combat value, unless they are converted to be unmanned aircrafts and used to be cruise missiles.

The most modern combat jets they have are Su-25, MiG-27 and MiG-29. Due to lack of replacement parts and fuel, the efficiency of those combat jet are not as good as those in the Russian air force.

North Korea has no aviation industry. They cannot manufacture aircraft parts. There is an issue they are worse than Iran is lack of jet fuel. There is no way the flight crew can get sufficient training.

North Korea don't have airborne early warning aircraft. Their anti-aircraft missiles and guns are seriously outdated. Back to 1960's China and Russia shoot down the American aircrafts with anti-aircraft missiles. Most of those missiles are SA-2 missiles. Today the North Korea still has a surplus of SA-2 missiles.

This is like using a time machine sending a Vietnam War communist air force to the 21st century. If there is a war against North Korea tomorrow, we could know the results before the war started.

A Paper Tiger: North Korean Navy

The situation of the North Korea Navy is better than their air force. North Korea have a ship building industry, they can take care the routine maintenance for their vessels. During the Cold War era China gave North Korea enormous assistance with ship building industry. They sold them enormous numbers of vessels. As a result, North Korea's navy today looks a lot like the Chinese navy back to the 1980's.

At that time, the Chinese navy was not as modern and refined as the Russian navy. The Russian navy was not as modern as the American navy. If you compare North Korean naval vessel to the American or allies navy, because the vessel they used are very different, a comparison is difficult to make. It would be easier to use a Chinese naval ship to judge the modernization and quality of the North Korean navy.

Everybody should know the North Korean navy is obsolete. To judge the degree of how obsolete it is: let's compare it to the Chinese navy:

North Korea have 70 submarines. The backbone of the submarine force are 22 Chinese-made Romeo-class medium submarine. Those submarines in the Chinese navy are all retired.

They also have older Russian made Whiskey-class medium submarine. China and Russia retired all the Whiskey class submarine several decades ago.

They have one or two Sinpo-class diesel electric submarine. Although the submarine is newly built the technology they have is equal to the 1960's China.

They have several dozens of Sang-O-class and 10 Yono-class midget submarines. Both of this kind of submarine are unreliable. There has been multiple incidents in the past that caused the deaths of some of its crew members.

After China stopped manufacturing Romeo-class submarines, later, started manufacturing Ming-class submarines. Today half of the Ming-class submarine are retired. After, they manufacture Song-class submarines. After they stop manufacturing Song-class submarines, they manufacture Yuan-class submarine. The Chinese submarine force is several generations more modern than North Korean ones.

North Korea does not have a cruiser or a destroyer. The biggest service combat vessel are three frigates, it looks similar to, but not exactly the same as the Chinese Janghu class frigates. During the 1970's and 80's, China built more than two dozen of Janghu class frigates. Today more than half of them are retired. During the 1990's China manufactured 14 Jiang wei-class frigates, some of them are retired. Today, the Chinese having 32 newly built Jiangkai-class frigates. The North Korean major surface ships are also several generations older than the Chinese's'.

North Korea has 31 missile boats. Excluding one new missile boat the rest of them are old Osa-class and Komar class missile boats. China and Russia retired all those missile boats for decades. In 1973 during the Yom Kippur War, the Arabs used those kind of missile boats to attack Israel. The Israeli navy sunk all of the Arabs missile boats who joined the battle. None of Israel's vessels were damaged or sunk. Back to the 1970's Osa-class and Komar class missile boats are already outdated.

North Korea has 200 torpedo boats, since anti-surface ship missiles used in war, torpedo boats have been outdated. China and Russia no longer have any torpedo boats in their navies.

North Korea has hundreds of fast attack crafts including gun boats and submarine chasers. Similar to 1974, were the Chinese naval vessels used in the battle of Paracel Islands. Those naval vessels for today's standards have no combat value. They could be used against pirates or illegal immigrants or smugglers.

In naval technology, a warship's guns and missiles are called 'hardware'. One of the very important parts is the surveillance and fire control systems. If a missile is fired at the enemy vessel, the sensors can be fooled by the enemy's electronic signals or decoys. The missile is not going to hit and destroy the enemy warship. In 1973, during the Yom Kippur War, the Arabs fired dozens of missiles at the Israeli Navy. None of them hit. The Israeli Navy fired missiles back and sunk all of the Arab's missile boats involved in the battle. It is a typical modern naval warfare.

The other technique against the incoming missile is to shoot it down. The North Korean warships almost have no anti-missile systems. Most of their naval guns are manually loaded with little to no chance to shoot down an incoming missile. The surveillance systems are pretty outdated. Because modern missiles are so fast, America or her allies can fire missiles at North Korean warships. Their naval anti-aircraft guns would not be able to respond before the missiles hits their vessels.

The North Korean navy have almost no anti-aircraft missiles. They don't have anti-submarine missiles either. All the naval technology are several decades behind China and Russia. The Chinese and Russian naval technologies is slightly behind America. How could they make threats of war against America? It could be a suicide mission if they dare start a war first.

A Paper Tiger: The North Korean Army

North Korea has a very large army of a million men and women serving active duty today. Including 100,000 Special Forces. They have 5,500 tanks, 2,200 infantry fighting vehicles, 8,600 large cannons/howitzers and 4,800 multiple rocket launchers. By the numbers it seems powerful. Actually it is not. Their air force and ground force look a lot like the Iraqi air force and army in early 1991 eve of the First Gulf War. There is a setback, the North Koreans lack food and fuel. The Iraqi military didn't.

There are those who worry about North Korean 100,000 strong special forces. This reminds me of Saddam Hussein's Republican Guard. When a powerful enemy approach they either die, run, or surrender.

I remember the days before the First Gulf War started, I watched TV and read books and magazines. Most people believe the coalition allied forces could defeat the Iraqi military with the price of heavy casualties. The end result was a surprise. The allies had only 358 military combat deaths, plus 776 wounded. The Iraqi suffer much heavier losses. 25,000 to 50,000 killed, 750,000 wounded plus 80,000 captured.

The real reason the allies were able to defeat Iraq so easily and with minimal casualties was because the Iraqi military systems a generation or older than the allies' weaponry. Today, several decades later, American's weaponries improved significantly. Excluding the use of nuclear weapons the North Korean weaponry systems are comparable to Iraqi's in the First Gulf War. If the American military can defeat Iraq several decades ago, there should not be harder to defeat North Korea.

In 1990, when Iraq invaded Kuwait it was a surprise attack. Kuwait is a small country with a much smaller army. As a result Iraq conquered Kuwait quickly.

Since the Korea War ended in 1953, South Korea has been on high alert to prepare the invasion from the North. Korea is a peninsula. South Korea only has one border, which is facing north. This border is called the DMZ, which is only 250 km long. Since it is the only border South Korea has, they can concentrate with their army just facing north. Since North Korea conducted several nuclear tests and firing long range missiles, they alerted the South Korean Government for a possible invasion. The North is not able to launch a successful surprise attack without South Korea's counter attack.

In ground warfare, there is a difference between offensive and defensive battling. If you want to invade another country, you need a much better military strength, including air support, heavy artillery, and armored vehicles. On the defensive side, they may not need a lot of heavy equipment. They can use guerrilla strategy, like how the Viet Cong fought the Americans.

To penetrate the enemy's defenses, there are several strategies. Sending a massive amounts of ground troops to directly strike the enemy's defense lines, having helicopters or military transport deliver weapons and soldiers behind the enemy's defense lines, or amphibious assault, landing soldiers on the enemy's coastline.

In the previous discussion, the North Korean Air Force and Navy consist of a bunch of outdated machines. If they dare to air drop their troops, most of their helicopters and transports would not survive before their troops land in the ground alive. The amphibious vessels and their naval vessels supporting the assault would mostly be sunk before the troops land. The only possibility is sending massive amounts of ground troops to launch a direct assault to the well-defended South Korean line.

South Korea has half a million active duty ground troops. In their inventory they have 2,500 tanks, 2,700 armored infantry vehicles and 5,800 heavy artilleries. The South Korean army is roughly half of the size of the North Korean army. Not just the quality of the South Korean weapons are much better than the North, the quality of life of the South Korean soldiers are much better.

The diplomates visited both Koreas and found something interesting, The North and South Koreans are the same race, why the South Korean soldiers are much taller than the North. Because of the lack of food and nutrition when growing up, but South Koreans are better fed. In recent years since North Koreas economy deteriorated, there were soldiers and civilians risked their lives to cross the DMZ. They escaped to the South. Somebody predicted is North Korean launch a military strike to the South, a number of their hungry soldiers would not fight the battle but surrender instantaneously.

Nobody will believe North Korea can possibly launch a successful ground invasion without air support. As soon as they attempt to cross the border, the weapons fired from the ground and from the air will cause large casualties, causing unbearable losses and forcing the North Koreans to retreat.

The human wave tactic, such as that used a few decades ago, is a mass suicide. Having tanks and armored vehicles launch a mobile assault, like what Nazi Germany did, is another option. Tanks and other heavily tracked vehicles use much more fuel than a civilian wheeled vehicle. Lack of fuel makes even the best armored force unable to claim victory.

In the most famous battle, Battle of the Bulge, Nazi Germany had much better tanks than the Allies. The heavy tanks, such as the Tiger, the Tiger II, and the Panther were by far superior to the commonly used Sherman tanks. The German tank guns could penetrate the frontal armor of a Sherman tank from a mile away. The Sherman tanks' guns were so weak, they were unable to penetrate the frontal armor of a German tank at any range. They could only penetrate the sides and the rear armor of a German tank at close range. In tank-to-tank combat, the Allies had to lose five tanks in order to destroy one German tank.

In the beginning of the battle, the Germans took advantage of the poor weather and the unpreparedness of the Allies and they defeated the Allies and penetrated the front lines. A few days later, when the weather improved, the Allies launched an air assault and stopped the Germans' offensive operation. At the same time, the German tanks ran out of fuel. The Germans' were unable to continue to fight much longer and retreated back to Germany. When the Allies recovered the territory occupied by the Germans, they found German tanks abandoned on the battlefield. They were not destroyed by the Allies but were, instead, destroyed by the Germans themselves after they ran out of fuel.

Through the experience of the Middle East conflicts, the quality of the armor of the Russian tanks are inferior to the American M1 tank's armor. The North Korean tanks, some imported from China and Russia, and some of them were made by their own, which are modified copies of Russian tanks. The South Korean tanks, some imported from America and a small number imported from Russia, some made by their own, which are modified copies of the American M1.

The gun barrel of the Russian 125mm tank guns are far inferior to the American 120mm tank guns. The armor piercing projectiles are also vastly inferior. Despite the 125mm tank guns having more charge in the chamber, since the charge they use is also more inferior to the Americans, the hitting power of the 125mm guns is less than the 120mm American guns.

During the Gulf War, there was tank-to-tank combat. None of the M1 tanks were destroyed by Iraqi tanks, and the American tanks destroyed hundreds of Iraqi tanks, and thousands by air strike, only a few M1 tanks were destroyed, either by friendly fire or blown up by a large landmine.

South Korea has much better military weaponry systems than the North. If North Korea would dare to invade the South, before the American sent more troops to Korea, the war may had been over and the South proclaimed its victory.

Korean Unification

In the previous discussion, I mentioned that I strongly believe Kim Jong-Un is a very brutal dictator but neither stupid nor crazy. He knows what would happen if he waged war against South Korea. He has no path to win the war but destroy himself and his own country. Recently, he has changed his tone and is now discussing denuclearization with the US and South Korea. He has also discussed the Korean Unification and invited President Moon Jae-In to visit Pyongyang. Obviously, the North Koreans have never planned to invade South Korea. This was only a threat.

Many newsmen have been fooled by Kim Jong-Un and were convinced that North Korea would soon abandon its nuclear arsenal and unite with South Korea. I predicted this will not happen. North Korea has a much smaller population than South Korea and is struggling in poverty and isolation. The situation is much worse than in East Germany during the communist occupation. The reason Kim Jong-Un has begun peace talks is to try to lift the sanctions and resolve the economic turmoil. He doesn't have the will to give up his nuclear arsenal and resign from his post.

Kim Jong-Un understands that he is a very unpopular tyrant and he is not willing to give up his power, knowing it could mean the death of him and possibly his whole family. Every communist leader politician will remember this famous story:

Shortly after Nicholas II, the last Tsar of Russia, was overthrown, his entire family was executed. He doesn't want to repeat this story because he know he is even less popular than the Tsar of Russia. He is not an elected government official who can just resign and become a regular citizen afterwards like the US presidents. His most powerful bodyguard is his nuclear arsenal. Of course, he's not willing to disarm his bodyguard.

One of the problems with the South Korean has a very advanced and democratic political system. The justice department is very independent. Throughout their history, the unpopular South Korean politicians, including several ex-presidents, have been impeached, ousted, and imprisoned. One of the most famous examples is Park Geun-Hye.

She is the first female president in South Korea and has the worst life of all South Korean ex-presidents. Both her parents died in separate assassinations.

In 1974, her mother Yuk Young-Soo, who was the first lady at the time, was assassinated by a communist. In 1979, her father Park Chung-Hee, who was the president at the time, was assassinated by his own body guard.

Since Park Chung-Hee was assassinated, several South Korean presidents were impeached or ousted. Their accusers believed that either themselves or their relatives involved were involved in corruption. In Eastern Asia, there is a very tight family relationship. Once a politician is put in power, his close relatives especially his siblings and children, will take advantage and pursue power themselves, and even accepting bribes. Although South Korea is stronghold of democracy, the old time caste system or family structure still persists. This kind of structure is called Neo-Confucianism, is an extension of Confucianism which is the Westerners don't not understand. The development of the Kim Dynasty which holds the philosophy based on Confucius ideals: "The nobility inherit power for generations. This is a set rule".

Below are several unlucky South Korean presidents accused of corruption:

1. When Chun Doo-Hwan was the President of South Korea, some of his relatives took advantage of his position and took bribes. Shortly after he left office, he and his relatives were arrested and he was sentenced to death. Along with taking bribes, he was also charged with treason. In South Korea, the maximum sentence for treason is death. Later on, his sentence was reduced to life in prison. His sentence was later commuted.

2. Roh Tae-Woo was also charged with taking bribes and treason was sentenced to 22 years in prison. Although his sentence was commuted, he was required to pay back the money he stole throughout his presidency.

3. Roh Moo-Hyun was the South Korean president between 2003 and 2008. As soon as he left office, several of his relatives were arrested for corruption and he himself was under investigation. During the investigation, he jumped off a cliff and committed suicide.

4. Lee Myung-Bok was the South Korean president between 2008 and 2013. Recently, he has been accused of taking bribes and abusing his power, has been sentenced to 15 years in prison, and is required to pay back the equivalent of $11.5 million.

5. Park Geun-Hye won the South Korean presidential election in 2012, and took office in 2013. In 2017, she has been accused of corruption and has been impeached and ousted. Recently she's been sentenced to 25 years in prison. Because she's already 66 years old, she will most likely die in prison.

Those cases, although not related in any way to Kim Jong-Un, makes him feel very uncomfortable. The South Korean Government has no way to guarantee any unpopular politician will not face dire consequences. This includes the top leaders, for Kim Jung-Un, who believed that he must stay in power or be ousted and suffer serious consequences.

One of the major problems are, North Korea is ruled by a dynasty. It is not a democracy. Any politician and once they are finished the term later returns to be an ordinary citizen. They are ousted, this means they can be killed or imprisoned. Their relatives could suffer the same consequences as well.

Kim Jung-Un has relatives who are also in power and are holding important positions. I am sure his relatives don't want to either be killed like the Tsar of Russia, or imprisoned for their lifespan, like Park Geun-Hye, they will advise Kim Jung-Un not to give up his power.

During the 2018 Singapore summit, Kim Jong-Un met with Donald Trump. He promised denuclearization. A few months after the meeting, there has been no evidence of them working towards denuclearization. Since the international sanctions are still in place, he put the blame on America. Recently, North Korea has again changed its tone. If the sanctions are not lifted, North Korea will keep and continue to develop nuclear weapons.

According to the most recent satellite image, North Korea continues to build up at least 13 missile launch sites, and estimating it could be up to 20 missile launch sites. The denuclearization proved this deception took place.

Zhuhai Air Show

Zhuhai Airshow is the largest air show in China. It takes place in the city called Zhuhai, which is near Hong Kong. In the most recent air show, the Chinese showed off some of their newest weapons systems. Although this show is called an airshow, naval and ground combat systems were the major exhibits together with aircrafts, missiles, and spaceships. To understand the latest military systems and armed trade policy of the Chinese military, this is the best resource.

The Zhuhai Airshow is open to the public. There is one show every two years. Since we can get the free information from public sites such as Google, I am not going to put down all the information into my book. I would like to have my opinion shared with my audience.

In a previous discussion, the Chinese Government does not support North Korea invading the South. Most modern Chinese weapons in this show can be purchased by foreign countries if the Chinese are willing to sell them. As an example, the Chinese sold FC-1 jet fighters to Pakistan (in Pakistan, this kind of jet fighter is named JF-17). You are not going to see North Korea, Iran, or Cuba purchasing this kind of jet fighter because the Chinese don't want to sell them advance jet fighters. The most modern military jets which are sold by China to Iran and North Korea are outdated J-7 jet fighters, which is a Chinese copy of the Russian MiG-21, which were exported decades ago. The most modern jets in the Iranian and North Korean inventory are the Russian MiG-29 jet fighter and Su-25 ground attack aircrafts. The message is do not worry about the Chinese selling modern military jets to both countries, but we may have to worry about the Russian arm exports to those countries.

One of the biggest surprises of the airshow is the Chinese introducing the CM-401 hypersonic anti-ship ballistic missile. Due to the international arm sale treaty not to export missiles with a range greater than 300km, the exported version of the CM-401 has the range limited to 290km. This is the downsized version of the DF-21D hypersonic anti-ship ballistic missile. The difference is either DF-21D or its successor DF-26 are the land based strategic missiles. They are too big to install in a destroyer. If they want to install this kind of weapon into the vertical launch system of a destroyer, they must downsize. CM-401 is the solution, and I'm pretty sure the missile used by the Chinese warships have much further range than the exported version.

This kind of missile works different from the traditional anti-surface ship cruise missile. When it fires to the sky, it climbs to its maximum height, which is too high for any ship-launched anti-aircraft missile to shoot it down. By the time it reaches the top of the enemy's warship, the missile increases to a maximum speed to strike the ship and penetrate its deck. The CM-401 missile could attack the enemy's ship at a speed of Mach 6. Currently, including America and Russia, nobody has the kind of ship-launched anti-aircraft missile that can shoot it down. When the North Korean propaganda swears they have the capability to sink an American nuclear-powered supercarrier, it is just unfounded communist propaganda. The North Korean strategic missiles are very primitive. They do not have the capability to manufacture the missiles like China does.

Hypersonic anti-ship ballistic missiles are the latest technology developed by the Chinese. Back to the Cold War era, the Russians used to study to use strategic ballistic missiles against enemy warships. Their mission failed. Today, China is the only country with this kind of weapon. Even America does not have any weapon similar to that. To sink an American nuclear-powered supercarrier is just other nonsense created by Kim Jong-Un.

A supercarrier battlegroup is a large nuclear-powered aircraft carrier surrounded by several heavily armed major surface ships. Those warships come with anti-aircraft, anti-submarine, and anti-surface ship weapons. It is hard to break through the defense line and sink the supercarrier. If the enemy fires conventional anti-ship cruise missiles, the early warning system of the carrier battlegroup would identify the missiles and shoot it down with long-ranged anti-aircraft missiles before they reach the inner defense ring. If missiles are able to survive, when it gets in the inner defense ring, the close-in weapons such as point-defense missiles and rapid fire anti-aircraft guns could take the missiles down. Of course, the electronic warfare system and decoys could also make the missiles lose their target. Today, only China and Russia have the military capability to sink a supercarrier.

There was another interesting communist propaganda that I found was false. Decades ago, I used to read a book stating that during the Korean War, a US heavy cruiser USS Chicago CA-136 was sunk by a North Korean torpedo boat. It is the biggest warship America lost due to enemy action after WWII and caused the deaths of hundreds of American sailors. In recent books published by the Chinese, you are not going to see this article anymore because they found that the statement was false.

Here is the facts: when the USS Chicago sailed close to the Korean coast, the North Korean torpedo boat squadron consisting of 4 torpedo boats attempted to sink the USS Chicago. The USS Chicago and her escorting destroyers opened fire on the North Korean torpedo boats, sinking 3 of them, with the last one escaping. It caused no damage to any of the American warships.

When the North Korean propaganda agency gave such false information to the Chinese, their books just published it this way. Until the Chinese found out that such statements were false, they just discontinued publishing these fake stories. Because North Korea doesn't have freedom of speech and press, the North Korean people still believe they were able to sink an American heavy cruiser. Now, they have to believe North Korea is capable of sinking an American supercarrier. But I believe this is just Kim Jong-Un's fantasy.

In North Korea, nobody would dare to mention about how the sinking of the USS Chicago is a lie because whoever mentions it and gets caught could be tortured to death. It is just like an old man making up a lie and telling it to his grandchildren. The old man says he was a hockey team leader and his team won a gold medal in the Olympic Games decades ago. The old man actually was not able to win gold, silver, or bronze, but he does know how to hit his grandchildren with a hockey stick.

Because of this lie, today the North Korean Navy is still equipped with 200 obsolete torpedo boats. In most of the navies on earth, the torpedo boats were all retired and replaced with guided missile attack crafts. They have no combat value, only serving as targets for the enemy.

In the airshow, one of the surprises is the Chinese high-tech anti-stealth surveillance system, including the long-range anti-stealth radar. In the previous discussion, the Chinese internet used to swear the radar system could detect an F-35 stealth jet as far as 350km away. Now they proved it is not a rumor.

There are J-20 stealth jet fighter which are comparable to the American F-22 which serves to show off their superior mobility. The model of J-31 medium stealth fighter is comparable to the American F-35, could become the next generation of the Chinese aircraft carrier warplanes is also on display.

There are many different kinds of unmanned drones on display. One of the biggest surprises is the CH-7, a stealth drone, which is a downsized B-2 stealth bomber. The CH-7 is capable of penetrating the enemy's air defense line.

C929 is the new generation jetliner, which is a joint developed project involving input from both Russia and China having a mop up displayed in the airshow. Of course, China and Russia are working together developing a series of weapons system. Due to its military secrets, few people know the select few details.

In the recent decades, the Chinese military technologies has improved significantly. In the past, when discussing Russian and Chinese military technology cooperation, the trade always went one-way, with the Russians selling the Chinese advanced weaponry and the Chinese paying money for it. Today, the tables are turned, and the Chinese have some modern weaponry that the Russians lag behind. For example, the stealth aircrafts, anti-stealth surveillance system, hypersonic anti-ship ballistic missiles, and AI technologies. Some of the most advanced Chinese systems have superiority over America and its allies. What would happen if China and Russia joined together in a military alliance? I am not worried the Chinese will supply modern weaponry systems to the anti-American countries such as North Korea, Iran, Cuba, and Syria, however it is possible that Russia might.

Since the Soviet Union collapsed, the Russian Navy also spiraled down with them. The sole aircraft carrier, the Admiral Kuznetsov, is out of service and is unable to finish retrofitting work because the folding dry dock sank in an accident. It has been suggested to have this aircraft carrier towed to China for repairs.

Admiral Kuznetsov is an older ship, built during the Cold War era. Its combat capabilities are drastically inferior to the American nuclear aircraft carrier. The Russians plan to eventually replace this ship. Due to tight financial standings and the technologies gradually becoming obsolete, it is a shadow program that never was actualized.

China has two conventional aircraft carriers in service. There are two aircraft carriers which are under construction. Both of these carriers are bigger than their predecessors. They are both equipped with cutting edge electromagnetic launched catapults, and at least one of them are nuclear powered. After these carriers are put in service they are to be equipped with stealth jets. There is a possibility that China will help Russia to build nuclear powered supercarriers, just like they helped the Chinese to build warships decades ago.

No Real War

In recent years, China has continued the process of constructing artificial islands in the South China Sea and has expanded its claims on the associated waters. America has refused to recognize the territories in the waters that are claimed by China. America has since challenged China through intentional trespassing by naval ships. The Chinese navy has tried to intercept the American intruders.

On September 30th 2018, the USS Decatur, an American destroyer, sailed within twelve miles of the Chinese occupied artificial islands. The Chinese navy deployed the destroyer Lanzhou to intercept this American warship. The Chinese warship approached the American warship with high speed and, suddenly, the Chinese ship changed direction and bypassed the American ship within 45 yards. This was a dangerous move and a near collision, which made the American destroyer change its path and left Chinese claimed territories.

Shortly after, retired General Benjamin Hodges, who used to be the former commander of the U.S. army in Europe, expressed his opinion. America and China will likely have a war within 15 years. Because of his title, he made headlines.

I worked with high ranking military personnel. This reminded me of the time I won an argument with Scott and other military men about China not supporting North Korea to invade the South. Also, an argument over Kim Jung-Un not having the will to start a war.

Don't let the titles General or Commander fool you. They are military men but they are not politicians nor economists. They had military careers as high-ranking, professional soldiers because they like to fight. There is a philosophy about careers: "If you have a career as a businessman, you must like money. Therefore, if somebody has a career as a professional solider, he must like to fight."

Unlike the former Soviet Union, the Chinese have no intention of invading other countries. They are interested in money, creating jobs, technology, and natural resources. America is the biggest cash cow for China in generating revenue and transferring advanced technologies. The South

China Sea contains the traditional Chinese territories. It possesses valuable natural resources, including oil.

Americans and other Westerners don't understand Chinese history. During the Ming Dynasty, from 1368 to 1644, China maintained continuous control of the South China Sea. The Ming Dynasty was a prosperous and magnificent era. It was the world's wealthiest nation and lone superpower. They defeated formidable Japanese samurais in Korea. The Dutch colonists were defeated in several sea battles. China developed a maritime silk road and also conquered colonies overseas in Vietnam and Sri Lanka. During the South China Seas conflict, reporters boarding the Chinese warships to ask the sailors questions would be told that the South China Sea has belonged to China since the Ming Dynasty and the Chinese sailors are just enforcing their duties to expel unlawful intruders.

There are two sides to every story. After the incident, the American media stated that they don't recognize the territorial rights of China in the South China Sea nor their right to stop American ships, stating the islands that the Chinese claimed as their own are just reefs or some rocks above sea level. They said it is not actual land, which is the entitled rights of a territory.

In Chinese military forums, some members say the Chinese warships are too lenient with the intruders. When they engage with the American warships, they should just capture the ships like North Korea captured the U.S.S. Pueblo in 1968 or just simply ram the American warship fiercely.

During the Chinese civil war, the communist Chinese naval vessels would capture the Chinese Nationalist naval vessels in the sea battles. Ever since then, the Chinese naval vessels have had their crews armed heavily with infantry weapons. A famous example was during the battle of Paracel islands in 1974. A Chinese minesweeper, after running out of ammunition for the main gun, the crews fired infantry weapons against a South Vietnamese destroyer. This was four times her size and claimed victory. This kind of battle tactic is called "the bayonet charge in the sea."

In recent history, the American navy did poorly in close combat in the sea. In 2016, the Iranian navy captured two American vessels, including the entire crew on board. The American crews surrendered without a fight. I imagine, if the Chinese ship Lanzhou launched the bayonet charge in the sea, they could have captured the USS Decatur. But the captain of Lanzhou decided to refrain.

During the Cold War era, there was a collision in the Black Sea involving the Soviet Union and the United States. In 1988, when the American cruiser USS Yorktown and the destroyer USS Caron sailed in close proximity to the shore, a Soviet frigate Bezzavetnyy intentionally collided with both American warships and caused damage. A Chinese warship would not have collided with an American warship but instead give out threats and warnings to leave the Chinese occupied waters or there would be a collision.

The Chinese react differently from the Soviet Union. The reason is very simple: the communist Soviets didn't have the trade and technology cooperation with America. If there were a conflict, they would have little to lose. The Chinese are dependent on the massive exports to America in helping their economy and creating tens of millions of jobs as well as gaining advantage of copying the American technology. Recently, the Americans started a trade war and posted tariffs on hundreds of billions of Chinese products exported to America. The Chinese lack the ability to retaliate and may possibly set a trade deal with America to end the trade war.

To prevent tens of millions of Chinese workers from losing their jobs, some Chinese companies are posting big discounts off their products exported to America and have lowered the value of Chinese yuan. As a result, tens of millions of Chinese factory workers can still keep their jobs. But the companies who export products to America made little to no profits. There is no evidence the trade war will become neither a Second Cold War nor a real war.

One major argument is that the Chinese rapidly increasing their military budget must mean they are preparing for war. Actually, in the past, the Chinese have spent too little on their military budget. The American government has a military budget bigger than the rest of the world added together. The Chinese military budget is roughly equal to a third of America's.

Since the Chinese have more money in the entire government budget, spending more money on the military is just a natural response. This is similar to a billionaire hiring more bodyguards when his business expands. He needs more security to protect his business. One of the concrete reasons China is not prepared for Second Cold War or a real war is because they only have approximately 300 nuclear warheads whereas America and Russia each have thousands.

I've read online that the Chinese only have 300 nuclear warheads (some sources say 260). I personally do not believe this because the number is too little. Many Chinese people post on the internet just like me. They do not believe the Chinese only have 300 nuclear warheads. One day, however, I read an article written by a Chinese official who gave a real, legitimate reason:

Nuclear warheads are very dangerous materials. After the Cold War ended, both America and Russia tried to disarm tens of thousands of nuclear warheads that expired due to long storage. Disarming the old, nuclear warheads is a dangerous and expensive program which poses a high risk of human deaths and injuries along with environmental destruction. When Russia tried to disarm the nuclear reactor of their retired nuclear submarines, there have been fatal accidents. We have no interest in starting either a real war or a Second Cold War against any country. If we don't use nuclear weapons, why would we need so many of them? By the time the weapons have to be retired and disarmed, disposing of the retired nuclear weapons would cause major hassles.

The artificial islands in the South China Sea serve as more than unsinkable aircraft carriers. They also service missile launched sites, weapons, fuel, food, and water depots and artificial harbors. To ask the Chinese to stop their projects is like telling America to stop building Gerald R Ford Class supercarrier. It is impossible for them to scratch the ongoing projects.

There are many countries that have animosity towards America. The biggest foes on the list are Iran and North Korea. Second in line are Syria, Venezuela, Cuba, and some other countries. Recently, due to Russia being accused of interfering in the 2016 election, the relationship between Russia and America has worsened. I believe the American Government should not be too hostile against the Chinese Government. If the situation worsens, we may soon discover countries such as Venezuela, Cuba, and Syria, which are recognized as American threats, equipped with anti-stealth radars and missiles, and/or hypersonic anti-ship missiles. Guess where the weapons and equipment come from?

Even though China does not directly sell advanced weapons or equipment to those anti-American countries, the Russians might and the Russians could get them from China.

Conclusion

When I was a little kid I remember there were rumors about WWIII. A lot of people believed the Warsaw Pact would launch a full scale invasion against NATO, conquer the entire Europe or even drop nuclear bombs on America. The history proves it is fraud.

In 1999, people worry about Y2K problems and believed all the computers would crash on January 1st, 2000. No such issues occurred.

There are those who believed that on December 21st, 2012 the world would end. Nothing of the sort occurred.

In the past several decades, there were tons of rumors spread by the publishers through books, magazines, and the internet, all of which are incorrect. The rumors say the Chinese Military will help the North Korean Military invade South Korea, including fighting the American Military bases in the West Pacific. Other rumors say China will launch an amphibious assault to take Taiwan. Some other rumor says China will have sea battles against Japan to take Okinawa. All of those rumors are unfounded in reality.

To discuss international conflicts is very similar to the weather forecast. If the weatherman says every day is sunny and nice, nobody would watch the weather forecast frequently. If the weatherman predicts hurricanes, damaging winds and thunder storms, more people would pay attention.

My news is too good to believe. There will be no war in the West Pacific in the next few years.

The sources concerning my book comes from decades of reading and memory. One of the sites that I read every day is https://military.china. com/ This site has a lot of subsections. The subsections of this site has a lot of information which is concerned about politics, history, military, and culture. The advantage about this site is they can link you to a lot of different professional Chinese sites. If you can read Chinese, you would be very surprised to see the impressions that the Chinese have of other people, including Americans.

Another sites I read frequently is https://lt.cjdby.net this is a popular Chinese forum.

www.ingramcontent.com/pod-product-compliance
Lightning Source LLC
Chambersburg PA
CBHW050409290526
45786CB00003B/1196